SCOTLAND
THE
FRAMEWORK
FOR CHANGE

SCOTLAND
THE
FRAMEWORK
FOR CHANGE

Editor: DONALD I. MACKAY

Paul Harris Publishing   Edinburgh

*First published in Great Britain 1979
by Paul Harris Publishing
25 London Street Edinburgh*

*ISBN Limp edition 0 904505 77 4
ISBN Cased edition 0 904505 76 6*

Printed in Great Britain by Bookmag Inverness

Contents

In Memory of John P. Mackintosh

Notes on Contributors

Donald I. MacKay, Professor of Economics, Heriot-Watt University. Author of a number of books including *The Political Economy of North Sea Oil* and *Scotland 1980*. Economic consultant to the Secretary of State for Scotland.

Carol Craig is currently Lecturer in Politics at Edinburgh University and undertaking research into Scottish local government.

Neil MacCormick, Regius Professor of Public Law, Edinburgh University; prospective Parliamentary Candidate (SNP) for Edinburgh North. Member SNP National Executive. Editor of *The Scottish Debate* (OUP, 1970).

John P. Mackintosh was MP for Berwick and East Lothian and Professor of Politics at Edinburgh University. He was author of *The British Cabinet* (1961) and many other works including *The Devolution of Power* (1968). He consistently urged the cause of devolution both within and without the Labour Party from 1956.

Alick Buchanan-Smith has been Member of Parliament for North Angus and Mearns since 1964. From 1970 to 1974 he was a Parliamentary Under-Secretary of State at the Scottish Office.

Henry Drucker, Senior Lecturer in Politics at Edinburgh University. Author of *The Political Uses of Ideology*, *Our Changing Scotland*, *Breakaway — the Scottish Labour Party*, *Doctrine and Ethos in the Labour Party* and Editor of *The Scottish Government Year Book*.

Geoffrey Smith is leader writer and political commentator on *The Times*.

Peter Jackson, Director of the Public Sector Economics Research Centre, University of Leicester, formerly of University of Stirling and HM Treasury. Joint author of *Public Sector Economics* published by Martin Roberston (1978).

James Kellas, Reader in Politics, University of Glasgow. Author of *Modern Scotland*, 1968 and *The Scottish Political System*, 1973.

James McGuinness (retired Civil Servant). Former Chairman, Scottish Economic Planning Board and Head of Regional Development Division, Scottish Office 1964-1972.

Stuart Page, formerly a serving Local Government Officer, and Senior Lecturer in Public Administration, University of Strathclyde. Currently visiting Research Fellow, University of Leicester, consultant to local authorities, and author of books on local government.

Desmond Misselbrook, Academic, Chairman and Director of Companies, Company Consultant, small farmer, Chairman of Livingston Development Corporation 1972-1978.

Preface

THE establishment of a Scottish Assembly will involve a major and possibly irreversible change in the form and manner in which Scotland is governed. It is not the intention in this book to support or oppose the creation of such an Assembly. Rather, for the purposes of analysis, it has been assumed that an Assembly will be established and on this basis that it is worthwhile considering what sort of animal it might be. The reader will find no recommendation to vote 'yes' or 'no' in the forthcoming Referendum but may find a better basis for an informed discussion of what might lie beyond the Scotland Act (1978).

Of course, even an Act as long and as boring as the Scotland Act cannot fully determine how any Assembly might develop. It will be a living institution which must respond to the political, social and economic pressures upon it and the Assembly will have to develop its own style and form of government to reflect its unique situation. For this reason, the main concern has been to set out the important features of the Scotland Act and to analyse the likely consequences for the internal organisation of the Assembly, its external relationships with the Secretary of State for Scotland, Westminster and Whitehall, intermediate government and local authorities, and the political parties. In each of these areas, the Scotland Act does not, and cannot establish, the precise manner in which the Assembly must operate. Inevitably, there is, and should be, scope for initiative and new action. The discussion points out the weaknesses in the Act, how these weaknesses might be modified, and also the directions in which the Assembly's own decisions will determine the results of this new form of government. Where necessary it speculates on the possible future development of the Assembly, although such speculation is rooted in an analysis of the balance of power which the Scotland Act appears to establish.

Each of the following essays takes the Scotland Act as its starting point. Throughout 1978 a series of discussions was held so that the working group had the opportunity to debate the substance of each of the following essays. The group represents many strands of political opinion and contains individuals with practical experience of politics, the Civil Service, and local and intermediate government, along with academics specialising in law, political science and economics.

Given the range of topics and opinions which are covered, no attempt was made to develop a consensus view. Nevertheless, a conscious attempt has been made to relate the discussion of different topics, so as to avoid duplication and to develop a common set of assumptions wherever possible. Each author remains responsible for his/her essay and for that alone, but the team assumed a collective responsibility for ensuring that the various topics are sensibly related and for ensuring that the discussion is not unduly partisan.

The project was financed by the Scottish Centre of Political Economy (SCOPE) established through the generosity of its Chairman, Andrew Ferguson, who took a full part in the work of the working group, but who disclaims any responsibility for the final product!

Finally, the book is dedicated to John Mackintosh who participated in the working group from its beginnings. His death was a cruel shock to us all, but it was typical of the man that his contribution was finished in typescript before the rest of us had begun to write. John Mackintosh was the major intellectual force behind the idea of devolution and we hope the book is not unworthy of his memory.

Chapter 1

Scotland: The Framework for Change

DONALD I. MACKAY

THE purpose of the essays contained in this book is not to advocate or propose the creation of a Scottish Assembly, but to describe and examine the nature and likely development of that Assembly should it be established. The technique adopted is to assume the existence of the Assembly, with the features set out in the Scotland Act, and to then analyse the powers of the Assembly, the nature of its relationships with other institutions and how these might develop over time. It is hoped that the discussion will help to promote a reasoned debate prior to the Referendum and, if the Assembly was then established, might provide some ideas and suggestions for its subsequent development.

The essays fall into three main categories, dealing successively with the framework proposed for the Assembly, its organisation and politics, and the likely implications for the various organs of government. Carol Craig and Neil MacCormick set out the powers proposed for the Assembly and the constitutional situation which is implied in these proposals. Following on from this, four essays consider the organisation and politics of the Assembly. John Mackintosh, in one of his last articles before his tragic and untimely death, argues for a strong legislature based on an effective committee system and Alick Buchanan-Smith sets out proposals for the Scottish Executive which attempt to combine efficiency and economy. Both essays are concerned with organisation and procedures but, as it is recognised that the devolution of power is basically a political exercise, the following two essays take up this theme. Henry Drucker discusses the implications for the political parties and Geoffrey Smith the relationships which may emerge between the Assembly and Westminster.

The remaining essays deal with the organs of government. Peter Jackson considers the question of financial responsibility and, as this is mainly concerned with the regulation of the Block Grant which is likely to be the centrepoint of negotiations between the Assembly and Westminster, provides the bridge between the essentially political relationships described by Geoffrey Smith and the formulation and execution of policy which is the day to day responsibility of government. James Kellas and James McGuinness discuss policy formulation and the process of administration, and Stuart Page and Desmond Misselbrook the likely interaction between the Assembly and local and intermediate government.

The Scotland Act does not propose the creation of a federal system of government in which each layer of government is sovereign within its own field of authority, but a scheme in which Westminster hands down certain powers to the Scottish Assembly which it will then exercise within resource constraints (the Block Grant) determined by Westminster and under the supervision of the Secretary of State for Scotland, Westminster retaining the power to override legislation proposed by the Assembly. The Assembly can amend or even repeal Westminster legislation which is within its area of devolved powers and, in practice, a quasi-federal system may emerge if Westminster respects the right of the Assembly to determine its own procedures and policies within its devolved fields and refrains from repeated or detailed intervention. However, given that the proposals have no obvious parallel in previous constitutional practice, it is difficult to draw any appropriate historical analogy. Instead, analysis has to depend on the particular provisions of the Act, interpreted in the light of the political environment in which the Act will be operated.

The lack of historical precedent is illustrated by comparing the manner in which power is to be devolved under the Scotland Act with the previous exercise in devolution following on from the Government of Ireland Act of 1920. The latter Act defined those powers which were to be 'reserved' to Westminster, so that powers not explicitly reserved were, by implication, transferred to Stormont. The Scotland Act stands this principle on its head, defining the powers to be exercised by the Scottish Assembly, so that any power not explicitly devolved is, by implication, to be exercised by Westminster. On some matters the division of power is clear enough. For example, Westminster is to retain responsibility for foreign affairs, defence, administration of justice and, in effect, will control all the important levers of economic power. While this is clear, many of the other demarcation lines are obscure and if demarcation disputes are to be avoided some method of policing such disagreements must be agreed.

The opening essay by Carol Craig explains the powers which are devolved under the Act and outlines the major sources of uncertainty which still exist. The bedrock of the Act is to retain to Westminster those powers which are considered necessary to the maintenance of the unity of the UK. This is considered to include, *inter alia*, the instruments of economic management, control of natural resources, internal security, international relations, the national framework of law and order and a raft of 'General Standards' covering areas of health and safety, common law and so on. One consequence of this method of devolving powers is that both Westminster and the Assembly often have a split legislative responsibility for policy areas — transport and education are two areas which come immediately to mind.

Basically, the Assembly is delegated powers which are largely confined to what might be called 'social legislation and policy'. This is a wide field, however, and an important one. The Assembly would be responsible in Scotland for most aspects of health care, social welfare policy, education, the arts, social and physical recreation, public sector housing, local government and finance, public passenger and freight transport services, tourist development, planning decisions relating to land use and development, criminal law, and civil law in so far as it does not affect company law, industrial relations and consumer protection. The legislative competence of the Assembly is most evident with respect to local government matters but even within this field major difficulties may arise because a number of local authority functions will remain the executive responsibility of the Scottish Office under the Secretary of State for Scotland. Indeed, the greatest difficulties may arise in practice from the relationship between the Scottish Executive and the rump of the Scottish Office, for, as Carol Craig demonstrates, undue complexity is introduced by continuing with legislative devolution not one, but two types of administrative devolution. As a result, the Scottish Executive will help administer laws passed both by the Assembly and by Westminster and work alongside another executive body in the shape of the Scottish Office under the Secretary of State for Scotland. This division of powers, and the problems which may arise from it, is taken up subsequently by a number of the other contributors and the general view appears to be that in time the balance of power will shift in favour of the new Scottish Executive, so that there will be a further diminution in the executive powers exercised by the Secretary of State for Scotland.

If the devolution settlement is to work it is essential to avoid jurisdictional conflicts, as the Assembly can only develop a consistent programme of legislation given a clear understanding of the area in which it can operate without intervention by Westminster. The Act,

against the initial intentions of the Government, has established a
judicial procedure in which the Judicial Committee of the Privy Council
ultimately determines whether legislation proposed by the Assembly is
intra vires or *ultra vires*. It is to be hoped that the judiciary will take a
liberal view of the Assembly's powers as was the case with Stormont.
Indeed, as Neil MacCormick points out, it is more important in the
Assembly case in that the confirming of power by affirmation subject to
a general negation, creates much greater room for conflict over the
boundaries between the devolved and non-devolved subjects than was
the case with Stormont. To avoid this possibility, and to create a
reasonable degree of freedom for manoeuvre on the part of the Assembly,
Neil MacCormick argues the case for a liberal interpretation of the
powers granted to the Assembly and suggests that such a liberal
interpretation has been the practice in Canada where the powers given
to the Provinces are granted by affirmation, as in the case of the
Scottish Assembly.

The Scotland Act, with minor and unimportant exceptions, leaves
the determination of its own standing orders and procedures to the
Assembly and these will be an important factor in determining the
balance of power between the legislature and the executive of the
Assembly. John Mackintosh's essay is a frank plea for a strong
legislature which will compel more open government than has been
customary in the UK. In this, he sees as the key factor the creation of a
committee structure reflecting the structure of the Executive, with a life
coterminous with the Assembly and combining legislative powers with
powers of scrutiny. The formal constitutional relationship is that the
executive is subordinate to the legislature, in that the former depends on
the continued support of the legislature which can also change the scope
of the powers exercised by the executive. In practice, party discipline in
the UK, reinforced by the electoral system, has created a situation in
which the executive has been dominant, able to command the necessary
majority in the legislature to transact its legislative business. It is
important to emphasise that when the Assembly is established the
initiative will lie initially with the legislature and not with the executive,
and the former will have a rare opportunity to establish its authority
vis a vis the executive. For example, if the Assembly wishes a strong
committee structure to be established it might be sensible to reverse the
usual procedure which, by first appointing the members of the
Executive, surrenders the initiative into its hands. Instead, the
Assembly might be better advised to first establish its committee
structure *before* choosing its First Secretary, thereby emphasising the

role of the committees in initiating and supervising legislation.

The structure of the Executive must reflect the nature of the powers devolved to the Assembly and the need for economy. The latter consideration, which should always be of first importance, has particular force given the unhappy, recent reorganisation of local government. A profusion of ministries encourages a profusion of expensive administrative posts and the extent of the patronage involved might allow the Executive more easily to control the legislature of the Assembly. Given these considerations, Alick Buchanan-Smith suggests that under the 'First Secretary' there should be a further seven ministers so that the structure of the Executive would be the First Secretary, Finance and Manpower, Development, Resources, Housing and Local Government Services, Education, Health and Social Welfare, and Legal and Home Affairs.

The devolution of power is a highly political process and should be recognised as such. The creation of a Scottish Assembly must have implications for the organisation of the political parties and clearly involves a change in the nature of the relationship between Scotland and the centre as represented by Westminster and Whitehall. The essay by Henry Drucker examines the first of these two themes via a discussion of the breakdown of the two-party system in Scotland, the permutations of party support in the Assembly which may be introduced by different electoral systems, the relationship between the 'British' and 'Scottish' elements within each party, the possible effect of policy initiation taken in Edinburgh on sectional interests, party organisation and party policy formulation, the relationship between parties and their elected representatives in the Assembly, including the selection of the leader of each party in the Assembly and the choice of candidates. Out of these issues it is difficult to determine which will be most important but, as far as the good government of the Assembly is concerned, the manner in which the parties formulate policies appropriate to Assembly government may be of crucial significance. At present, of the major parties, the Conservative's policy-making machinery makes the fewest apparent concessions to democracy, while the procedure adopted by the Scottish National Party is most elaborate and more subject to influence by the activists of the party. Yet the SNP have to face a new situation in that policies have to be framed in the knowledge that they may have to be implemented in practice, and the procedure adopted by the Labour Party, while it may appear reasonably open, is neither democratic nor particularly efficient. On the principle of 'he who pays the piper plays the tune', the parties in

Scotland may require to assert their financial independence of the centre if they are to make an effective break from past practice. The Conservative Party appears, at least formally, to have moved furthest in the other direction, but the Labour Party, too, depends on 'external' funds which is unlikely to be conducive to independent policy-making. Each party will face new pressures arising from the need to formulate policies for the Assembly and for Westminster, but, if the Assembly is to be effective, each must find a method of discussing and formulating policies with a specifically Scottish dimension. This fact alone may be a major catalyst for change within existing party machinery.

The efficient operation of the devolution settlement requires the development of a workable and reasonably harmonious relationship between the Assembly and Westminster. As far as the efficient conduct of government business is concerned this will require, Geoffrey Smith argues, a close relationship between the Scottish Executive and Whitehall, a role which can best be filled through the Scottish Office. Equally important, the Assembly and Westminster must each recognise some limits on the extent to which they push disagreements and this will require concessions on both sides. From the Scottish viewpoint the most immediate question is likely to be the number of Scottish MPs at Westminster, and for Westminster the most difficult issue is likely to be the qualification of the doctrine of ministerial responsibility at the centre which is implicit in the proposed scheme. That is, while the devolution settlement is based on the principle that Westminster can enforce its will through the Secretary of State for Scotland and its override powers, it must mean, if it is to work in practice, that Westminster MPs will have to recognise a limit on their power to raise questions and initiate debate on devolved matters. As was the case with Stormont, a convention will have to be developed wherein ministers are not held to be responsible for replying to questions which relate simply to the conduct of the Scottish Assembly in devolved areas. The Scotland Act involves, as Carol Craig has shown, a number of areas of possible overlap and ambiguity between what are devolved and non-devolved subjects and early practice, particularly the rulings of the Speaker, are likely to be of crucial significance.

Initially, the nature of the relationship between the Assembly and Westminster will be dominated by the negotiation of the Block Grant, for on its size and manner of composition will depend the financial freedom of manoeuvre granted to the Assembly. The Government's proposals are that the Assembly will receive a Block Grant voted by Parliament, this grant including local authority Rate Support Grant. The Scottish Executive must pay Rate Support Grant to local authorities in Scotland, but the proportion of the Block Grant to be distributed in this form is a matter at the discretion of the Assembly. As to the Block Grant itself, the White Paper, *Devolution — Financing the Devolved Services* (Cmnd. 6890) lays down that its size shall be determined by an assessment of Scottish needs relative to the needs of the remainder of the UK. This is self-evident but some set of operating principles for determining the size of the Grant must be established and major difficulties could ensue.

Peter Jackson outlines two possible models of Grant determination. The first, what he calls the 'centralist model', is that the Scottish Executive will be required to explain and account for variations in the standard and provisions of devolved services as compared to the equivalent English services. Such detailed control would inevitably make it difficult to depart from the English pattern, whether or not it suited Scottish conditions. Other possibilities do exist, so that under a 'co-operative model' some simple rules would determine the size of the block grant without unduly inhibiting the ability of the Assembly to determine its own priorities on devolved matters. This is of crucial importance. Historically, Parliament's control over the executive rested on its control over finance. An equitable solution demands that Westminster should ensure that the size of the Block Grant for Scotland is related, through some set of agreed principles, to the level of similar expenditures in England, but there Westminster's responsibilities should end. It is the Assembly's responsibility, and its alone, to determine the allocation of the Grant so determined.

Thus far the discussion has been largely concerned with the Assembly, particularly its legislative function and its relationships with the Scottish Executive and with Westminster. Such a preoccupation is understandable enough, but it may tend to overlook the possibility that the success of devolution may depend on the ordinary day to day business of government which is dependent on the Executive. As James Kellas observes, the Assembly may be 'master in its own house' but the Scottish Executive is not. Unless some simple general principles for determining the Block Grant are applied, the Executive will be forced into conformity with English standards. It will have the responsibility for administering laws passed by the UK Parliament in subject areas which are particularly sensitive in Scotland (land use, development, pollution) and it is in relation to the exercise of the Executive's powers that the so-called 'Governor General' aspects of the Secretary of State for Scotland's role will be most evident. The Act will establish two administrations in Scotland — the new Scottish Executive and the rump of the present Scottish Office under the Secretary of State for Scotland — with closely related functions. The Executive, given its reliance on the Block Grant, the overriding need to satisfy the Secretary of State for Scotland and its dependence on the Scottish Office in its intermediary role with Whitehall, appears to be the weaker. So the answer to the provocative and highly pertinent question posed by James McGuinness, 'Who will be Scotland's top Civil Servant?', might appear to be the permanent Under-Secretary of State at the Scottish Office. Certainly the Scottish Office will retain many significant powers — the negotiation and monitoring of the Block Grant; the administration and development of the Scottish interest in retained functions; the maintenance of effective liaison with UK departments operating in Scotland and a continued interest in the economic issues affecting Scotland. It will be necessary and desirable, at least initially, to build up the authority and influence of the Scottish Office in Whitehall if it is to act as an effective intermediary. In the longer run, however, as the Scottish Executive and its constituent departments acquire legitimacy and authority in their exercise of administrative responsibility, and in their accountability to the Assembly for the devolved services, it seems probable that its administration will acquire a distinctive style and character of its own and indeed become a separate Civil Service with its own aspirations and career structure. In that event, the relationship between the Scottish Executive and the UK Executive may become increasingly direct and inter-governmental in character so that the Scottish Office may prove, as James Kellas suggests, to be one of the first organs of governments to fulfil the historical prophecy that it 'will wither and die'.

The group have had very much in mind the unease which has so often been expressed over the reorganisation of local government. Local government reorganisation has been criticised on two main grounds. First, that the new, larger authorities have made local government more 'remote' and second, because it is suspected, not without some justification, that the costs of reorganisation in terms of the personal aggrandisement associated with new posts, new staffs and new offices, may have outweighed any 'economies of scale' which might have flowed from the creation of larger authorities. Yet there were clear difficulties in operating the previous system of local government with many extremely small authorities, and a concern over present arrangements does not justify a wholesale return to the historical pattern.

This is emphasised by Stuart Page who believes that the nature of the functions which are carried through by local government required the creation of larger units, but that the further centralisation involved in removing powers from the regions to the Assembly would not be justified. No blueprint for any further reorganisation of local government is laid down, nor does the essay suggest a new radical reform is desirable. What is desirable is that greater thought should be given to the nature of the functions which local government should discharge and the implications of these for the appropriate level of local and/or Assembly government. Specifically, Stuart Page suggests that it was a mistake to reject the Wheatley recommendation that housing should be a regional service, and that the current and shared powers with regard to leisure, recreation and planning, together with the regional supervisory role which accompanies them, has aggravated the difficulties which have arisen from jurisdictional disputes and functional overlaps. The present division of powers between districts and regions seems to encourage fragmentation and factionalism while creating considerable public confusion as to where responsibility lies. For this reason alone some reform seems certain to follow on from the creation of a Scottish Assembly. Another major reason lies in the working relationships which are bound to emerge between local authorities individually and collectively, and the Assembly. With the continuance of the interest of the Scottish Office in certain matters affecting local government, and a UK presence in the social and economic development of Scotland which has a local government dimension, the injection of a new level of government into the traditional central/local relationships is bound to bring under critical scrutiny the whole machinery of local government and its role in the new structure created by the Assembly and its administration.

Intermediate government includes those advisory, regulatory and executive functions carried through by bodies which are appointed, directly or indirectly, by central government. That some intermediate level of authority is necessary in certain circumstances cannot be seriously contested, for it allows government access to expert advice and permits the creation of bodies with executive and regulatory powers in areas where day to day management activities are required. It would be unreasonable and expensive to insist that these functions should always be discharged by the Civil Service which often has neither the professional skills or the managerial know-how to carry through the required range of tasks. Yet, recent concern over intermediate government is typified by the increasingly outspoken attacks on the proliferation of 'Quangos', the acronym for quasi-autonomous non-government organisations. Underlying this is the view that the present system of intermediate government is unduly expensive, inefficient and is fundamentally undemocratic.

As Desmond Misselbrook observes, there is a real danger that this concern may result in throwing the baby out with the bath water. He is particularly concerned to safeguard those institutions, above all the New Towns, which have been responsible for attracting new enterprises and encouraging new investment in Scotland. Few would disagree with the proposition that proved institutions should not be disturbed for the sake of change and many would accept that the New Towns have played a prominent and valuable role in restructuring the Scottish economy and in bringing about a necessary redistribution of population. Again, it is difficult to seriously contest the view that the New Towns are, and are likely to remain, attractive locations for new industrial development. Nonetheless, the reorganisation of local government and the creation of the Scottish Development Agency does require some thought to be given to the relationship between these agencies and the New Towns and, even if the end result is to confirm the role and powers of the latter, it is desirable this should be considered by the Assembly. Further, the Assembly is bound to be concerned with appointments to intermediate government which presently are made in a manner which is clearly liable to political manipulation without proper consideration of candidates on their merits. It is difficult to avoid the uncomfortable feeling that the present method allows the executive arm of government undue patronage, which could be used to reward the faithful, or to buy the acquiescence of those who would otherwise be more critical of existing policies.

The essays cover such a wide area that it is not possible for a mere editor to do justice to their contents. For the main part each essay has to be read for itself. Yet from the brief review above and from the essays themselves, three main points emerge and impinge on all or most of the separate contributions. These are, the manner in which power has been delegated to the Scottish Assembly, the supervisory function of the Secretary of State for Scotland and the negotiation of the Block Grant.

With regard to the first of these, the manner of delegating power to the Assembly creates substantial difficulties. The alternative method of devolving powers, of specifying the powers reserved to Westminster, would have created a more clearly delineated and broader area within which the Assembly would have functioned. Unfortunately, while this is still a possibility for the future, the attempt must be made to work the present system of devolved power by affirmation subject to a general negation. In order to establish a reasonably firm basis for Assembly legislation it is crucial, as Neil MacCormick suggests, that the process of judicial review should be based on 'a large and liberal view of the provisions of the Act' and also that Westminster MPs are prepared to observe the spirit of the devolution proposals, which is to remove an area of government from their immediate purview. It is the latter which may be the more difficult to ensure, and yet it will be the more crucial. The principle underlying the Scotland Act may be that 'power devolved is power retained', but an attempt to continue Westminster supremacy in devolved matters would be highly undesirable in practice. If devolution is to be effective Westminster has to recognise a clear distinction between devolved and non-devolved matters. That is, following the Stormont principle, a convention needs to be established that UK ministers are not responsible for matters devolved to a Scottish Assembly and, in turn, this requires that MPs should recognise a limitation on their ability to raise questions and initiate debate at Westminster.

The second major theme is the role of the Secretary of State for Scotland and of the remaining rump of the Scottish Office. If the Scotland Act is put into force the executive powers of the Secretary of State will be much diminished, but the Secretary of State will have a supervisory role *vis a vis* the Assembly. He will be able to demand information from the new Scottish Executive as to the exercise of their powers and, with respect to bodies such as the Scottish Development Agency and Highlands and Islands Development Board, will establish guidelines within which devolved powers will be exercised. Again, the Secretary of State will be responsible for monitoring Assembly legislation and, indeed, has the power to override that legislation in certain circumstances. Where it is considered that the Assembly may be trespassing outside its defined area of competence, the Secretary of State can refer the matter to the Judicial Committee of the Privy Council for decision. Finally, the Secretary of State and the remaining rump of the Scottish Office will continue to be the channel of communication between Edinburgh and Whitehall. The power of the office of the Secretary of State for Scotland will undoubtedly be diminished *vis a vis* Whitehall, but his position remains, at least in theory, an extremely powerful one relative to the new Scottish Executive and legislature. It is these powers and their possible exercise which have coined the title 'Governor General', and in this context this suggests that the Secretary of State will exercise more than simple ceremonial powers!

The supervisory powers given to the Secretary of State for Scotland are quite sweeping and may appear to betray some lack of faith in the basic principle of devolution. James Kellas argues that the major weakness of the Scotland Act is the failure to create a strong Scottish Executive and that the Executive will be highly dependent and subservient to the UK Executive. Certainly, there is a marked contrast with the Government of Ireland Act of 1920. The latter Act established a Northern Ireland Civil Service but did not require the creation of an Irish Office or the post of Secretary of State for Northern Ireland. That is, the Government of Ireland Act could be said to be much closer to 'Home Rule' than anything implied by the Scotland Act.

The short-run situation created by the Scotland Act is evident enough. The Scottish Executive, if it is to be effective, must work through the Secretary of State for Scotland and what remains of the Scottish Office. As a number of essays point out, this will require a strengthening of the Scottish position in Whitehall. This may provide a stable solution, but the long-run position is nothing if not problematical. An alternative possibility is that the office of the Secretary of State for Scotland will decline in influence and importance because it is shorn of most of its executive functions. If so, there may be an increasing tendency for the Scottish Executive to approach Whitehall and Westminster directly, on what Kellas calls a government to government basis. The logical outcome of this development would be a situation akin to that created by the Government of Ireland Act, namely a movement to a single administration responsible for its own Civil Service.

The third important factor which is touched on by many of the essays is the procedure for negotiating the Block Grant. Two potential causes of conflict need to be avoided — a situation where the Scottish Assembly could blame all deficiencies on Westminster parsimony, and also the other extreme, where Westminster could, through its control of the Block Grant, effectively determine the distribution of devolved expenditure within Scotland. Scottish expenditure on functions which are to be devolved has amounted previously to 14.5% of equivalent English expenditure. Over time this percentage has been quite stable and does not depart markedly from the venerable Goschen formula of 11/80ths. Presumably this relationship is meant to reflect an equitable solution and there is the practical consideration that it cannot be changed substantially without a major change in the quantity and quality of Scottish services following hard on the heels of devolution itself. Hence the starting point for devolved expenditure is fairly clearly defined, but it is still necessary to develop some method of determining future expenditure.

The White Paper, *Devolution — Financing the Devolved Services* (see Cmnd. 6890) lays down that the size of the Block Grant shall be determined on an assessment of Scottish needs relative to those in the remainder of the UK. The White Paper states: 'It is clearly desirable that discussion of the appropriate level of devolved expenditure should be informed to the greatest possible extent by objective data and a mutual understanding of needs and problems. Studies are now being undertaken within Government Departments with the aim of collecting objective information on needs and standards of public services in all four countries of the United Kingdom. The Government hope this information will help them and the devolved administrations to make informed judgments on levels of expenditure and to explain them publicly.'

As Peter Jackson observes, the White Paper can be interpreted in different fashions, but the main difficulty is that the Scottish Executive might be required to explain and account for variations in the standard and provision of devolved services compared to equivalent English services. Such detailed control would inevitably make it difficult to depart from the English pattern, whether or not it suited Scottish conditions. One possibility would be the creation of an independent advisory body to collect and analyse information and assess relative needs, but there would be a real danger that such a body would effectively dictate policy. Such a suggestion does not meet the point that the Assembly itself should be the ultimate judge of the pattern of expenditure within the Block Grant allocated to it. In short, the Assembly should be able to proceed with a course of action contrary to both the wishes of Westminster and of any advisory body, so long as such expenditure is on a devolved matter and within the overall Block Grant. To achieve this it is necessary to determine the basic principles which should determine the Block Grant and these principles should satisfy the following criteria:

1. They should be reasonably simple so that they can be generally understood.
2. They should be equitable between different regions.
3. They should take account of such special features which may influence the cost of providing services to certain standards.

4. They should create a situation where it is not possible for either the Assembly or Westminster to easily affect the size of the Block Grant and, yet, they should reflect changing circumstances over time.

It is impossible to meet these criteria in full but, in the spirit of Geoffrey Smith's contribution, we should not let the best be the enemy of the good.

Indeed, it is possible to apply a modified type of Goschen formula which would go a long way to meeting these various requirements. For example, the starting point for determining the relationship between Scottish and English expenditure on devolved matters should be the relative populations of the two countries, as it is only equitable to insist that expenditure must have some relationship to the size of the population being served. Further, in the interests of equity, all government taxation and expenditure systems attempt to favour those groups with relatively low incomes. In other words, any expenditure determined on a *per capita* basis should be supplemented by a further allowance reflecting differences in *per capita* income, so that expenditure *per capita* on devolved services would be higher in those parts of the UK with lower *per capita* income. Further modification could occur if, for example, the demographic structure of the respective populations effected the level of expenditure considered desirable, or if other special factors were at work. Thus, allowance could be made for a situation where Scotland or England had a relatively high proportion of persons in older or younger age groups requiring special help with respect to the provision of social services, education etc. Again, allowance could be made for the provision of services in regions where geography and topography create relatively high costs. The obvious example, as far as Scotland is concerned, is the Highlands and Islands and there are strong strategic grounds for maintaining a certain mimimum level of public service in this type of area.

A Goschen-type formula, based initially on respective populations and further weighted for difference in *per capita* incomes, demographic structure, and the special factors associated with sparsely populated areas, could certainly produce a division of expenditure on devolved functions close to that presently prevailing. If such a formula could be agreed it would have certain further advantages. First, the way in which devolved expenditure was arrived at could be fairly easily understood. Second, it would be extremely difficult for the Assembly or for Westminster to effectively change the size of the Block Grant, because to do so requires operating on variables such as population, age structure, *per capita* incomes etc. which are not amenable to easy influence by Parliamentary bodies. By way of contrast, consider a situation where the size of the Block Grant was based on a detailed assessment of needs. If, for example, the assessment of needs included allowance for one-roomed houses, houses with outside toilets etc. then it would always be in the Assembly's interest to maximise the number of houses of these types in order to maximise the size of its Block Grant! It could be said that the Assembly would have an interest, under the criteria herein proposed, to reduce *per capita* income in Scotland. It is difficult to believe that such a move would be electorally popular or, fortunately, that the Assembly would necessary be successful in this direction, even if it tried! Third, the size of the Block Grant in Scotland relative to the Block Grant in England would change over time, given a change in respective populations, *per capita* incomes, age structure etc. This is as it should be, but the rate of change would be likely to be slow, given that the relationship between these variables changes almost imperceptibly over time, and this would provide reasonable stability for long-term budgeting.

The main advantage of the above method of determing the Block Grant is that it would preserve the freedom of the Assembly to determine its own priorities within its defined area of competence. It illustrates one way of helping to ensure that the real transfer of power accompanies the trappings of office. Indeed, the following essays demonstrate that the method in which devolution could work is not set in aspic by the Scotland Act. Many important issues remain unresolved. The Act represents only the first step in a major reform of the constitution of the UK in which practice and experience will prove more powerful than the initial instrument. The following essays have been written to clarify what the Act often appears to obscure, but above all to promote a better, informed discussion of the alternatives which lie behind the constitutional reform as proposed.

Chapter 2

The Powers of the Scottish Assembly and its Executive

CAROL CRAIG

WE cannot hope to understand how Scotland will be governed after devolution unless we know what an Assembly and its Executive are empowered to do. But despite the importance of understanding the demarcation lines of government institutions and functions, the division of powers is one of the most complicated aspects of the Scotland Act.

In view of the volume of existing legislation there is no easy way to delineate an Assembly's powers. Nevertheless, the Government seems to have adopted the most difficult approach. In devolving power to an Assembly, there are two main ways in which its legislative competence can be defined — either by stating what will be retained by central government or by outlining the powers of the devolved body. When setting up Stormont in 1920 the Government of the day adopted the former approach, but in 1978 the Government has chosen a hybrid solution to the delineation of powers. The Act lists under twenty-five separate headings groups of devolved matters, indicating in only the most skeletal fashion what these groups include. It then expressly exempts certain matters which are to be retained by Westminster. As this is followed by a seventeen-page list of enactments and 'whether or how far' these are included in the devolved groups, a full understanding of what is devolved depends on knowing what these enactments contain.

In the next chapter, Neil MacCormick spells out the constitutional implications of such an approach but here it is necessary to make two simple observations. Firstly, if matters are not mentioned then they are 'reserved by silence'. This means that over time the Assembly will not automatically acquire new powers unless they fall quite clearly within the groups of devolved matters. In other words, Westminster will have to make a decision to devolve more powers. Secondly, the lack of clarity and precision in the Scotland Act means that in the first few years of an Assembly's existence much time will have to be spent testing out and establishing the areas of legislative competence.

Bearing in mind the difficulty in defining precisely what is devolved and what retained, this chapter will outline the powers which have been devolved to the Assembly and its Executive. It will also indicate how the devolved institutions may find their activities circumscribed. Two preliminary observations are necessary. Firstly, the Scotland Act provides for the Assembly to have full legislative competence over certain matters and for the Scottish Executive to be responsible for their administration. However, there are a number of areas in which the Assembly is to have no legislative power, yet the Scottish Executive is to have responsibility for the execution of Westminster's legislation or policy. An example of this is abortion. Originally, the Assembly was to be given the power to legislate on abortion but this was deleted in the final Parliamentary stages of the Bill. However, although the Assembly is to have no legislative power the Scottish Executive is to be responsible for the administration of the 1967 Abortion Act or any subsequent piece of Westminster legislation. This leads us to the second point. In order to clarify the separation of executive from legislative power, in this chapter the term Assembly is used in those instances where there has been devolution of legislative power. Thus although, as James Kellas points out, the Scottish Executive as a Government will be responsible for the formulation of policy and the initiation of major legislation, the Scottish Executive is only referred to where the Assembly has no legislative power.

The Powers of The Scottish Assembly

It is always difficult to tabulate succinctly and clearly areas of government activity, but for the sake of brevity this is what the following table attempts to do. It lists the main subjects contained in the twenty-five groups of devolved matters and sets beside them related powers which have only been executively devolved. Under the heading 'non-devolved' are listed a number of matters which one might have expected to fall within the devolved groups but which are retained by Westminster.

SUBJECT AREA	MAIN MATTERS DEVOLVED		MAIN NON-DEVOLVED MATTERS RELEVANT TO GROUPS
	LEGISLATIVELY & EXECUTIVELY ONLY	EXECUTIVELY ONLY	
HEALTH	Almost all aspects of health care including — Structure and operation of the NHS Policy on and supervision of private practice and nursing homes Contraception Ethical questions such as transplant surgery and use of dead bodies Investigation of maladministration	Abortion	Control of food, drugs and medicines Occupational health Medical schools
SOCIAL WELFARE	Social work services including those affecting — Children (e.g., adoption and Children's Panels) The handicapped The elderly Groups in need of special care and support (e.g., alcoholics) Supervision of standards of private provision Allocation of grants to voluntary bodies		Social Security and related benefits Disabled persons employment Sheltered employment

EDUCATION, THE ARTS, LIBRARIES ETC	School education — structure, standard and attendance requirements including the school leaving age. Curricula development. Policy on private education.	Grants to Universities under the Education (Scotland) Act 1962	University education
	Nursery education		Research Councils
			Career guidance
	Higher and adult education		Student grants (university, teacher training and HND)
	Youth & Community		Carnegie Trust
	Teaching profession		
	Cultural and recreational activities		
	The Arts		
	Museums, Art Galleries and libraries (includes both buildings and the acquisition of material)		
HOUSING	Public sector housing including allocation of public funds and subsidies	Local Authority Guarantees of Housing Loans	Private housing finance
	Rent control, rent allowances and rebates in both public and private sector		
	Upkeep and improvement of all accommodation		
	Mobile homes and caravans		
	Building standards		
	Slum clearance		

SUBJECT AREA	MAIN MATTERS DEVOLVED		MAIN NON-DEVOLVED MATTERS RELEVANT TO GROUPS
	LEGISLATIVELY & EXECUTIVELY	EXECUTIVELY ONLY	
LOCAL GOVT. & LOCAL FINANCE	Structure of local government including control of constitution and boundaries for both electoral and administrative purposes		Voting system, frequency of elections, voting & membership qualifications
	Allocation of Rate Support Grant		A number of local government functions (e.g., consumer protection and traffic wardens) are not devolved.
	Calculation of rates levy (could alter how this is determined but not replace it with a local income tax)		
	Pay and conditions of service of local authority employees in devolved subjects		
	Investigation of maladministration		
TRANSPORT	Provision of and subsidies for passenger transport by bus, boat and rail other than B.R. (i.e. the Glasgow Underground)		Anything affecting transport as an industry rather than as a service (e.g., vehicle standards)
	Licensing of bus routes		Public service vehicle licensing
	Subsidies to B.R. for passenger services		Freight service licensing
	Provision of and subsidies for road freight operated by the Scottish Transport Group		British rail
	Air freight subsidies to meet a special Highland need		Air services and freight services other than STG

	Aerodromes (e.g. approach roads, by-laws, acquisition of land, public health, noise, vibration, insulation of buildings)		Air traffic regulations
			Pollution from aircraft
	Inland waterways (Although legislative competence on aerodromes and inland waterways is devolved, this will have little practical effect until the Secretary of State, on request by a Scottish Secretary, makes an order under section 69 of the Scotland Act adjusting the responsibilities of the British Airports Authority, the Civil Aviation Authority and the British Waterways Board.)		Major ports
	Marine works (improvement, provision and maintenance of minor piers and boatslips)		
ROADS	Construction, planning and standards of roads, including motorways	Regulations affecting the movement of traffic on all roads except motorways	Legislation relating to traffic management
	Road safety publicity		Motoring offences
			Traffic wardens

SUBJECT AREA	MAIN MATTERS DEVOLVED		MAIN NON-DEVOLVED MATTERS RELEVANT TO GROUPS
	LEGISLATIVELY & EXECUTIVELY	EXECUTIVELY ONLY	
PHYSICAL PLANNING & THE ENVIRON- MENT	Most planning decisions relating to land use and development which have only local or regional importance. This includes —	Some land-use and development powers	Some parts of the Community Land Act are totally reserved
		Aspects of pollution control	
	town and country planning; New Towns; environmental improvement; protection of countryside amenity and landscape; water, river management and sewerage; environ- mental functions of the SDA		Forestry
	Erosion and flooding		
	Pollution (but not of cars, aircraft or dumping at sea) and noise control		Powers relating to compensation for compulsory purchase and the procedure for making and approving compulsory purchase orders
	Ancient Monuments (e.g., appointment to Boards, listed buildings, grants)		
	Miscellaneous land-use powers such as those relating to allotments, burial and cremation, markets and fairs, sport and recreation, refuse collection and disposal		
FISHERIES	Freshwater/salmon and migratory trout fishing — protection, improvement and maintenance — within fixed esturial limits		Seawater fisheries

	Powers listed under marine works in Transport group	
AGRICULTURAL LAND	The power to acquire and manage land and provide and equip agricultural holdings. This includes management of agricultural holdings presently in the hands of the Secretary of State for Scotland.	Agricultural policy (e.g., agricultural price support system and research and development)
	Landlord/tenant relationships	Agricultural wages
	Crofting (including payment of grants, loans and subsidies)	Forestry
TOURISM	Matters relevant to the development of tourism in Scotland	
HOME AFFAIRS & MISCELLANEOUS MATTERS	Fire service	Betting and gaming
	Public holidays	Taking of censuses of the population
	Shop hours and the regulation of local trades	Game licences
	Lotteries	Petroleum spirit licensing
	Charities	
	Registration services including population statistics and archives	
	Some licensing (e.g., dogs, liquor, places of entertainment)	

SUBJECT AREA	MAIN MATTERS DEVOLVED		MAIN NON-DEVOLVED MATTERS RELEVANT TO GROUPS
	LEGISLATIVELY & EXECUTIVELY	EXECUTIVELY ONLY	
LAW & LEGAL SYSTEM	Civil Law		Law relating to non-devolved subjects (e.g., taxation, road traffic offences, employment and company law)
	Criminal Law		
	Legal Profession		Matters affecting security of state (e.g., treason and terrorism)
	Legal Aid, Advice & Assistance		Police
	Treatment of Offenders (e.g., Prison Service)		Prerogative of Mercy
	Tribunals relevant to devolved subjects (e.g., Rents Tribunals but not Industrial Tribunals)		Appeals from Courts of Session to House of Lords
	Courts (e.g., juries and contempt of court)		The right of the Court of Session and the High Court to regulate their own procedure and that of inferior courts
	The Scottish Law Commission		Appointment of Judges and Sheriffs

An easy target for any potential critic of the Scotland Act is the division of powers. Even at first glance there appear to be a number of anomalies. Social welfare, for example, is devolved but the employment of disabled persons is not; education is within the powers of the Assembly yet Westminster retains control of careers guidance. However, by examining the criteria for devolution and reservation of functions set out by the Government in its White Paper *Our Changing Democracy* (Cmnd. 6348) it is possible to discern some method in the apparent madness of the Scotland Act.

As the Government is proposing devolution, and not independence or federalism, it is not surprising that the major criterion for the reservation of power is the preservation of the economic and political unity of the United Kingdom. In order to maintain economic unity the Government retains control over the management of the economy, including such matters as the tax system, interest rates, social security, currency, regional policies and the public sector. Thus although social welfare is devolved, social security and related benefits are not. Likewise, although health and education fall within the legislative competence of the Assembly, the reservation of employment explains why such matters as occupational health and careers guidance are kept within Westminster's control.

With the aim of preserving the political unity of the UK, the Government keeps a number of other powers. These are powers necessary for national security, international relations (including, of course, all matters stemming from Britain's membership of the EEC) and 'the national framework of law and order, guaranteeing the basic rights of the citizen throughout the UK'. It is within this context that we must understand the Government's decision to reserve control over the police and the electoral system.

Under the heading 'General Standards' the Government also outlines an entire legislative area which is not devolved. And it is with reference to this criterion that we can understand a large number of minor exemptions such as food and drug control and vehicle standards, which otherwise seems to fall within the groups of devolved matters. The Government maintains that there are a number of functions where 'common rules and standards are important for safety or to maintain a fair and consistent framework for industry and commerce everywhere.' This covers most of the work undertaken in Scotland by the Regional Councils' Consumer Protection departments but also includes matters ranging from company law to shipping and civil aviation regulations.

Reservation of functions according to such principles may be sound in theory but in practice lead to fragmented policy-making. Such fragmentation could affect both the Assembly's and Westminster's approach to planning and policy formulation. Transport provides a good example of how a detrimental split in responsibility may occur after devolution. The Assembly is to have substantial powers with respect to roads and transport provision but the Government's decision to reserve the nationalised industries means that it will have no control over British Rail. Thus, while the Assembly is to be responsible for the overall planning of bus routes, its only hope of being able to determine passenger rail services is dependent on its ability to offer financial inducements to B.R. — a power, incidentally, that local authorities currently have. The Assembly will not even have this power with respect to rail freight services. In effect this means that the Assembly will find it difficult to formulate an integrated transport policy for Scotland. Even if we accept that it is necessary to preserve the unity of the nationalised industries it, nevertheless, seems feasible that a scheme could have been devised whereby B.R. has to submit its investment plans for Scotland to both the Scottish Executive and the Minister of Transport. This would have allowed the Executive more room for negotiation and consultation with B.R. about Scottish services and given them more of an opportunity to plan transport services in Scotland.

Westminster's complete control over B.R. may seem unnecessary but it at least accords with the basic principles underlying devolution or reservation of functions. But this is not true of other areas in which fragmentation of policy may occur. University education, for example, was not devolved because many senior academics and officials were hostile to the proposal. And given that the Assembly is to be responsible for schools and for certain aspects of further and higher education, the reservation of the universities may result in failure to develop an integrated education policy. The Government in *Our Changing Democracy* recognises the need for collaboration between the various educational bodies but justifies its proposal by maintaining that post-devolution it will be possible to devise suitable administrative arrangements with the University Grants Committee.

The reservation of forestry presents a further example of how fragmentation may occur, in this instance in the management of agricultural land and in land-use planning. Unlike university education, however, forestry was originally scheduled for devolution in the Scotland Bill. It was deleted in the final Parliamentary stages after the Commons accepted a Lords' amendment to this effect. This deletion, it appears, was the result of pressure from forestry interests who were mainly hostile to the devolution of their industry. The non-devolution of forestry seems similar in this respect to that of the universities — the major difference being, however, that forestry interests were forced to argue publicly the case the universities presented privately.

But let us leave the question of fragmentation and assess the significance of what is devolved. It is certainly paradoxical that despite the link between dissatisfaction with Scotland's economic performance and the demand for devolution, the Assembly is to have no revenue-raising powers and no direct control over employment and investment matters. Control of resources such as oil, coal and sea fishing is likewise not devolved. However, it is overly simplistic to claim that only economic powers are important; that the Assembly will be an expensive but irrelevant addition to the government of Scotland. Yet this is what is frequently believed. Even pro-devolutionists, in arguing the case for an Assembly to have economic powers, have tended to play down the significance of what is actually devolved.

In essence, the matters within the legislative competence of the Assembly are such that its decisions will inevitably affect the quality of people's lives. It has control over most significant aspects of law and social policy and through its planning and land-use powers its decisions will largely determine the face presented by both urban and rural Scotland. As the Assembly is to have a wide range of powers in these policy areas, its existence will profoundly affect the operation of voluntary bodies; not only is it likely to become the focal point for the lobbying activities of such groups but also many of them will become subject to the Assembly's control. Indeed, the Assembly will be responsible for the regulation of charities, the allocation of grants to voluntary bodies and for the standard of any care or support they provide in the social welfare sector.

On the whole, the impact of devolution will be felt less through actual legislative change and more through the way in which the Assembly allocates the resources at its disposal. In theory at least, in allocating the Block Grant it will ultimately be responsible for deter-mining priorities in the devolved areas. Thus, for example, it will decide how much money should be allocated from the Grant to subsidise the Arts. Incidentally, this money could be allocated to various artists and institutions either directly by the Assembly itself or through the Scottish Arts Council or similar kind of body. The Assembly will also decide how money should be allocated within the devolved subjects. Take health, for example: by adopting a new policy on health, it could switch resources from patient care to preventive medicine.

It is certainly the case, however, that there will always be direct or indirect restrictions on the Assembly's policy options. As various authors in this book point out, the Assembly's freedom of action could be curtailed by the way in which the Block Grant is negotiated. On other occasions, the Assembly's policies could be restricted because matters relevant to the subject area have not been devolved. If we take our health example a stage further we shall see that an Assembly, although pursuing a policy of preventive medicine, may find that as it has no powers with respect to employment a major course of action is prohibited. In other words, although acknowledging the link between occupation and illness an Assembly could not, under the terms of the Scotland Act, establish an occupational health service aimed primarily at preventing occupationally linked disease. Yet it is often argued that this is the kind of direction health care should take in future years.

The Assembly's potential inability to adapt its policies in harmony with contemporary developments may also be seen in housing. The Scotland Act devolves public sector housing to the Assembly but Westminster retains control over private housing finance. This accords with the Government's intention to keep control over such economic matters as interest rates. Fortunately, the non-devolution of this aspect of housing is at present moderated by the fact that approximately 54% of all Scottish households are in the public sector. However as all political parties, including Labour, are coming to favour housing policies which emphasize private housing, the Assembly could soon find itself bereft of significant housing powers.

The Assembly may find its policy options restricted in other ways. Of crucial significance here is, of course, the Secretary of State's power to refer an Assembly bill to Parliament if any of its provisions either directly or indirectly affect a reserved matter. An example of such potential intervention may be found in the Assembly's responsibility for the school leaving age. Although the Assembly could if it wished lower this from 16 to 14, the Westminster Government could, with some justification, argue that in releasing so many school leavers on to the job market the Assembly was affecting employment — a matter which is not devolved. A further example may be found in housing. The Assembly has legislative power over rents, yet in exercising this power it may seriously affect any counter-inflationary measures taken by Westminster. It must be emphasized however, that although

Westminster will always have the legal right to intervene in such cases, on many occasions it would be politically unwise to do so. For instance, the policy adopted by the Assembly may have been included in the majority party's election manifesto, thus allowing the Executive to portray its actions as embodying the wishes of the Scottish people.

Another body who may restrict the Assembly's freedom of action even in devolved fields does not spring so readily to mind — it is the European Convention on Human Rights. As Lord McCluskey pointed out recently, although devolution makes the treatment of offenders a purely Scottish matter we may come to see 'that power diluted by rulings of non-elected international jurists'. Indeed, as he also indicated, such supranational rulings extend beyond the treatment of offenders, covering other legal matters and such questions as the use of the belt in schools and even the vaccination of children. This is not a problem of the devolution proposals, however, as it affects representative political institutions throughout the world.

Members of an Assembly may be indignant that their freedom of action will be curtailed by external bodies, but the very existence of an Assembly is likely to restrict other bodies, such as Scottish local authorities. Although a subsequent chapter in this book examines the relationship between the Assembly and local government, a number of observations are pertinent at this point.

If we look at the various subject areas within the legislative competence of the Assembly, we shall see that most of these are local government matters. Although local authorities have increasingly become the administrative arm of central government, a new and probably zealous Assembly is likely to restrict even further the opportunities they have to take important decisions. For example, the Assembly may wish to legislate to guarantee council house tenants certain rights. However, in many of the subject areas under the control of the Assembly, significant change will be dependent less on legislation and more on the allocation of resources to priority areas and on decisions regarding the administration of services. In short, as these are precisely the kind of matters which could be dealt with at length in Assembly committees, the Assembly may pressurise the Scottish Executive to interfere with local authorities.

Post-devolution Scottish local authorities will become servants of the Assembly. As their master, the Assembly will have control over their constitution — the general rules relating to meetings and proceedings — and be responsible for their electoral and administrative boundaries. (This does not of course include any matter relevant to electoral law.)

In having effective control over the allocation of local authority functions an Assembly could, if it wished, abolish the Regional Councils, transfer functions from one tier to another or totally restructure local government in Scotland. It could also put matters such as health, currently administered by regional boards, under local authority control.

The Assembly's relation to local government is, however, complicated by the fact that although it is responsible for its structure and finance, a number of local government functions are not devolved. The most significant of these matters are police, food and drug control, consumer protection, ports, some licensing powers and traffic wardens. This means that by restructuring local government the Assembly could affect the administration of a non-devolved matter.

More important than this implicit power to affect non-devolved subjects is the fact that complex sets or arrangements will have to be devised to accommodate this split in responsibility for local government matters between the Assembly and the Scottish Office. Arguably, it is the retention of a number of local authority functions which will make devolution unduly complicated and difficult to administer. Moreover, even if we accept that these matters should not have been devolved legislatively to the Assembly, there seems to be little reason why the Scottish Executive could not have been given responsibility for their administration. After all this is the arrangement which has been devised for a number of other matters. But let us leave in abeyance the question of extending the powers of the Scottish Executive and concomitantly of depleting the administrative functions of the Scottish Office, until we have examined the powers which have only been executively devolved.

The Powers of The Scottish Executive

Schedule II of the Scotland Act lists 'matters within powers of Scottish Executive but not within legislative competence of Assembly'. The significance of the powers devolved in this way varies dramatically. At one extreme there is the very insignificant power contained in the executive devolution of small sections of the Race and Sex Discrimination Acts pertaining to educational establishments in Scotland. There are also a number of powers from the Community Land Act which are very significant to planning decisions. But undoubtedly the most important powers to be executively devolved are those relevant to industrial development functions. Such powers are contained in this schedule, others in section 42 entitled 'Industrial and Economic Guidelines'. Let us look first at what the guideline function involves.

Post-devolution, the Secretary of State for Scotland 'with the approval of the Treasury' will prepare guidelines for the exercise of various industrial and economic development powers within Scotland. Various bodies like the Scottish Development Agency already work to guidelines set by the Secretary of State. For example, guidelines for the Agency are issued to ensure that, like the National Enterprise Board, it observes what are considered to be 'proper standards of commercial behaviour'. Target rates of return, minimum interest rates and so on are also set for the Agency and contained in the guidelines. After devolution, however, the Secretary of State for Scotland will issue the guidelines to the Scottish Executive and the relevant Scottish Secretary will then issue them to the appropriate agencies. In other words, it will be the job of the Scottish Executive 'to give effect' to the guidelines by assuming responsibility for their implementation and enforcement. The Secretary of State will, of course, always have the power to intervene if these guidelines are not issued by the Scottish Executive or observed by the various agencies.

The Scotland Act outlines three areas of activity which will be subject to such guidelines. The first of these is the industrial development functions of the SDA. The Act states that SDA functions relating to 'the promotion, financing, establishment, carrying on, growth, reorganisation, modernisation or development of industry or industrial undertakings' will be the subject of guidelines. The second broad area for guidelines is the economic development functions of the Highlands and Islands Development Board. And the final area is the disposal of land or premises for industrial purposes. Such guidelines will therefore affect the work undertaken in Scotland by the SDA, the HIDB, local authorities and the New Town Development Corporations.

Reports on all guideline functions will be presented to Parliament and to the Assembly.

It seems that the Government was forced to adopt this guideline scheme to help solve a problem inherent in its devolution proposals. The problem is essentially one of fragmentation of responsibility. The Government wants to retain control over industrial development and regional policy. It does not, for example, believe that Scottish institutions, such as the SDA, should be able to affect adversely the interests of other parts of the UK by offering more generous forms of assistance than is available elsewhere. However, complete Westminster control over such matters raises problems since some devolved subjects, such as land-use planning and New Towns are obviously related. This difficulty is amply illustrated with reference to the SDA.

The functions of the SDA fall into two broad areas of activity — environmental matters and industrial investment. According to the Government's criteria for devolution, the first is within the Assembly's legislative competence while the second is to be retained by Westminster. In effect this means an inevitable split in responsibility for the activities of the SDA. In *Our Changing Democracy* the Government proposed to get round this problem by having the Secretary of State appoint half the SDA board members and, after consultation with the Assembly's administration, its Chairman. The splitting of the board's appointment in this way was widely criticised as unworkable and so a new scheme had to be devised.

The scheme proposed in the Scotland Act is based on executive devolution of the industrial investment functions of the SDA. Thus, as long as the Scottish Executive give effect to the guidelines set down by the Secretary of State, it will ultimately be responsible for this aspect of the SDA's operations. As the Assembly has full legislative power over the environment, derelict land and factory building the devolved institutions have responsibility for most of the Agency's activities. Such responsibility is reflected in the proposals for financing and appointing the Agency post-devolution. For those functions for which the Assembly and its Executive have some responsibility (i.e., including guideline functions) the Scottish Executive will decide how much money will be allocated for their execution. The allocation will then be made from the Block Grant. Although the Scottish Executive cannot abolish the Agency or change the nature of the Board's composition, it will be responsible for the appointment of Board members.

It is important to note, however, that a few of the SDA's functions have not been devolved either to the Assembly or its Executive. These are the promotion of industrial democracy in undertakings which the Agency controls and the powers of 'selective financial assistance'. The latter are powers under section 7 of the Industry Act 1972. Related to this is the reservation of the appointment of the Scottish Industrial Development Advisory Board. In essence, the reservation of this power means that any financial assistance to industry which is out of line with the terms set out in the guidelines, can be given by the Agency only on the direction of the Secretary of State for Scotland.

So far the guideline functions and the relationship of the Assembly and its Executive to the SDA have been outlined. Given the importance of the SDA we must ask if this scheme gives the Executive any real power. In other words, is it merely window-dressing — an attempt to put the SDA under the apparent control of the devolved institutions without a real shift in decision-making — or does it reflect a genuine move on the Government's behalf to concede more power than it originally intended?

Despite the importance of the question it is too early to give a definite answer. Much depends on how the scheme works out in practice. All that is possible at this stage is to draw up a list of things which may be weighted in the Executive's favour.

First of all there is the question of finance. The allocation of SDA money from the Block Grant may give the Scottish Executive an important say in the extent of industrial investment in Scotland. However, given that we do not know as yet exactly how the Block Grant will be determined, in practice the power to allocate money may mean nothing at all.

Secondly, there is the Scottish Executive's power to appoint the Board and its ultimate responsibility for the operation of the Agency. Although in the normal course of events the Agency will make decisions as to the exercise of its powers, the Executive's relationship to the Agency, particularly its powers of patronage, will ensure that it does not step too much out of line with any policies the Executive wishes it to pursue.

This leads us to the third factor in the Scottish Executive's favour, and that is the fact that section 4 of the Scottish Development Agency Act 1975 has been devolved to the Executive, thus empowering it, in the industrial investment area, to give the Agency 'directions of a specific or general character'. In other words, if all else fails, it could tell the Agency what to do. The Secretary of State for Scotland currently has the power to give directions to the Agency but has used it only once since the Agency's inception. It is unlikely that a Scottish Executive would use this power more readily since its indirect control of the Agency would usually be sufficient. It must also be remembered that any direction given by the Executive would have to comply with the terms of the SDA Act, with the powers devolved to the Scottish Executive and with the content of the guidelines.

A factor obviously weighed against the power of the Scottish Executive in industrial investment matters is the Secretary of State's responsibility for the formulation of the guidelines. Although consultation may take place (e.g., in the proposed Joint Councils) between the Scottish Executive and the Government on what the guidelines should be, all such consultation will take place on a purely non-statutory basis.

However, if the guidelines continue to be drawn up on the same kind of basis as at present, this will give the Secretary of State only negative power. In other words in a sense he can tell the Agency what it cannot do but not what it must do. Nevertheless it is possible that after devolution these guidelines could be more tightly drawn and stimulate in detail the nature of the Agency's activities. But this is unlikely since the guidelines are generally similar to those set for the NEB.

The power to give selective financial assistance, however, is obviously very important to industrial investment and will always maintain the Secretary of State's significance in this field.

If we take all these factors into consideration it appears, however, that on balance, significant control over industrial investment in Scotland has been devolved, via responsibility for the SDA, to the Scottish Executive. It must also be remembered that a similar kind of scheme has been devised for the Highlands and Islands Development Board. The Assembly will have legislative power over the Board's social development functions and the Executive will have responsibility for other aspects of its activity. As with the SDA, the Scottish Executive will appoint the Board — but it cannot abolish it or amend the boundaries for its activities — and will allocate money for its operations from the Block Grant.

The benefits of the guideline scheme may, however, be paid for in other ways. A Conservative Government at Westminster issuing the guidelines and a Labour Scottish Executive being required to give them effect illustrates, for example, how this solution to previous problems may well be a 'recipe for conflict'.

Moreover there are bound to be occasions when there is confusion over responsibility for guideline functions. If an elector is dissatisfied, say, with an aspect of the SDA's activity which is the subject of guidelines, to which sets of politicians should he or she turn: to the Assembly member who is ultimately responsible for the way in which the Scottish Executive is using its power or to the Westminster MP who is responsible for the economic strategy on which the guidelines are based?

The splitting of responsibility for guideline functions between West-minster and the Assembly certainly presents problems of accountability and intelligibility. As such a problem is inherent in any split between executive and legislative powers, it may arise in all areas in which the Scottish Executive is charged with the administrative responsibility for aspects of Westminster's policy or legislation. But despite this it may be preferable in the long run to extend this form of devolution to a number of other functions; by extending executive devolution, to eliminate completely the administrative functions of the Scottish Office.

The Role of The Scottish Office

It has already been argued that the non-devolved local government functions could and should be handed over to the Scottish Executive. This would leave only a few functions to be administered by the Scottish Office — agriculture, sea-fishing, oil development, the SSEB and a few economic planning powers being the most significant. Arguably these few functions could likewise be devolved to the Scottish Executive. In effect this would mean the complete abolition of the Scottish Office. Although the post of Secretary of State for Scotland would remain, he would have no responsibility for the actual adminis-tration of functions. His department would comprise a small back-up staff dealing with matters relevant to his 'Governor General' powers *vis a vis* the Assembly, and to the formulation of policy for subjects which have only been executively devolved. This department would also draft any specific Scottish legislation required for subjects administered by the Scottish Executive but not within the legislative competence of the Assembly.

Certain advantages and disadvantages would accrue from the elimination of the Scottish Office. On the debit side is a very important political consideration. Given the likelihood that the post of Secretary of State will automatically decline in importance with the advent of the Assembly, the complete erosion of the administrative functions of the Scottish Office would probably make it even more difficult for the Government to justify his place in the Cabinet. And, in view of the non-devolution of economic powers and control of resources to the

Assembly, this could present a serious threat to Scotland's ability to protect its economic interests at Westminster.

On the credit side, however, it must be emphasised that by eliminating the Scottish Office in this way we would greatly simplify the political process in Scotland. Such a simplification is required not for the sake of administrative tidiness but for political intelligibility. The complicated nature of government in Scotland post-devolution will largely be due to the co-existence of legislative devolution with *two* kinds of administrative devolution: there will be an Assembly making laws with a Scottish Executive administering these laws *and* some other laws passed by Westminster; and there will be the Scottish Office operating on a different form of administrative devolution. If we remember the other tiers of government — Regional and District authorities and the EEC — and the fact that Westminster's input into government in Scotland will be channelled via central departments like the Department of Employment, via the various activities of the Scottish Office and via the Scottish Executive, we realise how confused even the most informed Scottish citizen is likely to be. The removal of the Scottish Office as an administrative unit would thus do something to simplify the picture. It would help solve the split in responsibility for local government functions in Scotland and make the Westminster dimension of government more intelligible.

In short, under the terms of the present scheme, a likely obstacle to public understanding of the political system post-devolution is its complexity; for appreciating its mechanics and demarcation lines will become a major task. This may add to the work of political scientists and educators but will do little to decrease the remoteness of government or increase the extent of participation in public life. And isn't that what devolution is all about?

Chapter 3

Constitutional Points

NEIL MACCORMICK

Introductory

THERE is, as it were, an official prejudice in Britain against 'written' constitutions. Oddly enough, although the United Kingdom of Great Britain was founded by a written instrument, the articles of Union and the relevant Scots and English enabling legislation of 1707, the official view is that there is not and never has been any written constitution of the UK. Those who heap the grandest praises on the Union and its architects inexplicably discount its constituent status.

Written or not, the fundamental principles of the British Constitution are simple enough and well understood. The highest legislative authority is vested in the Queen in Parliament, and governmental power of an executive kind may be exercised only within the limits set by common law or statute law, any of which may be varied by subsequent Act of Parliament. The ultimate arbiters of every legal issue are the superior Courts of Scotland, England, and Northern Ireland, including the House of Lords as a common final Court of Appeal for some, though not all, matters. Apart from any possible doubt as to the alterability of fundamental terms of the Articles of Union, the judicial function is to interpret and apply, not to review, the law as laid down by Parliament. All this is simple, readily intelligible and pretty widely understood.

Intelligibility of law, especially constitutional law in its fundamental principles, is a great good. It is an all but necessary condition of political democracy and civil liberty.

But the grand simplicities of the Constitution are, *vis a vis* Scotland at least, greatly qualified by the enactment of the Scotland Act 1978; or they will be if the Act is brought into effect after the Referendum for which it provides, 40% rule and all.

For the authorities constituted by the Act, it is in the full sense a written constitution — it constitutes them and fixes their powers, yet it is not alterable by them. Their powers being fixed by law, they may not transgress the fixed limits of the law. If they do, judges will review their actions and nullify them to the extent of the transgression; and so on.

The justifying ground of the Act is a democratic one: that the manifold operations of government in Scotland deserve and require effective democratic control and scrutiny; there is an implicit subsidiary justifying ground of nationalism with a pretty small 'n', to the extent that Scotland as such is reckoned an appropriate unit for the operation of the democratic principle.

By way of declaration of position, it should be said that the present author's own strong convictions are on both counts in favour of implementing the Act and of voting 'yes' in the Referendum; this despite a long-run preference for a far more extensive form of self-government for Scotland than that which the Act envisages. But these points will not be argued in this essay. The concern of the essay is to review the main outlines of the Act from the viewpoint of constitutional law; the prime concern being with the Act as establishing an interlocking set of powers which are to operate within the overall system of the existing British Constitution.

By way of a general preliminary, it must be said that if the case for having an Assembly depends on and is justified by democratic principle, nevertheless to have one at all entails some necessary sacrifice of the principles of simplicity and intelligibility: two-tier legislation and government is more complex than one-tier. To favour devolution at all is to accept some such sacrifice. But it is a discussable question whether the Scotland Act succeeds in minimising any necessary sacrifice of intelligibility. It will be suggested that the Act does not so succeed, and that it is to that extent defective in principle.

Suffice it here to record the opinion that no better Act could have been forthcoming from Parliament in present circumstances or any likely circumstances of the near future. The present choice is devolution on these terms, defects and all, or no devolution. What seems likely is that if the Referendum records a 40% 'yes' majority and the Act is brought into effect, there will be further evolution and the possibility of improvement; at least of tidying up more obvious defects and inelegancies in the Act.

But the purpose of this essay is neither to predict nor to advocate such future changes. The first requirement is a simple review of the

Act as it stands, and the structures which it creates; a tall enough order for an essay of this length.

I

The Scotland Act 1978 establishes two new legal entities: the Scottish Assembly and the Scottish Executive, and it confers on them significant legal powers: legislative powers and executive powers. The Act envisages, without expressly ordaining, that the exercise of these powers and the interrelationship between them will be governed by conventions similar to those which operate in the current British Constitution. That is to say, the executive power will be subordinate to the legislative in at least two senses: first, since executive power may be validly exercised only in accordance with law, the legislature can, by changing the law, change and control the scope of executive power; secondly, since the condition of appointment to executive office is capacity to command the confidence of the legislature, it follows that in matters of political judgment, the legislature in principle controls the executive, whose power is conditional on retaining the confidence of a majority in the legislature.

As every schoolboy knows, however, these propositions cannot be adequately understood without reflection on the dynamics of the political system which focuses upon the Constitution. Modern politics being party politics and modern government being party government, the legally superior power of the legislature tends to be negated by the politically superior position of the executive. The leaders of the majority party in Parliament can normally rely upon party discipline and political partisanship to secure that the majority in the legislature gives the executive its head.

Further qualifications need to be made about the specific relationship which will obtain between legislature and executive within the purview of the Scotland Act.

First, not all of the laws which authorise the Scottish Executive to act are subject to the legislative authority of the Scottish Assembly. Schedule 11 of the Act lists a considerable range of 'Matters within powers of the Scottish Executive but not within legislative competence of Assembly'. These matters include, for example, certain powers of making grants to Universities, and certain powers in relation to the Highlands and Islands Development Board and to the Scottish Development Agency — the nearest approach in the devolutionary scheme to a devolution of power in relation to industry and the economy.

Here, then, we have an area of executive power which, though conferred and defined by law, derives from laws made by and changeable only by the UK Parliament.

Secondly, and not unrelated to the above, the Assembly will be neither the only nor the highest authority which can scrutinize, criticise and demand changes in policy decisions by the Scottish Executive. A British Secretary of State (presumptively, but not by legal definition, the Secretary of State for Scotland) may intervene and reverse decisions of the Scottish Executive, or impose other decisions, in the areas of devolved power, as is discussed in section III below.

Apart from that, it is not clear that the Assembly's formal authority over the Executive does or can mirror that of the UK Parliament over the UK Government. The formal power of appointment to 'secretarial' (i.e., 'ministerial') office in Scotland is to rest with 'the Secretary of State'. He will appoint as 'First Secretary' whomsoever, if anyone, the Assembly nominates for the office. Failing such nomination he will no doubt (as does the Queen at the UK level) offer appointment to someone whom he thinks able to sustain the confidence of the Assembly; other 'Scottish Secretaries' will be appointed on the First Secretary's advice, and all will hold office 'at Her Majesty's pleasure'. Thus, they will be dismissible by the Queen on the advice of her (UK) ministers.

We may presume that the power of dismissal will be exercised when, and only when, Secretaries severally or jointly lose the Assembly's confidence. But, since the provision for dissolving the Assembly and calling an election before the end of a four-year term is to operate only when, by a majority of two-thirds, the Assembly resolves for its own dissolution, the consequence of an Executive defeat on a motion of confidence will not be the same as it normally is at Westminster. There is no guarantee of an immediate or early election, and no certainty that a new Scottish Executive established after dismissal of the former one will enjoy a normal working majority.

It may well be the case that this will increase the political influence of the legislative Assembly over the Scottish Executive, because of the absence of anything paralleling the British Prime Minister's right to request and normally to be granted a dissolution of Parliament. It is certain that the conventions which must evolve around these constitutional arrangements will differ in some measure from the parallel conventions at Westminster.

It should not be forgotten that a historical source of the power of Parliament, and more particularly of the House of Commons, as against the Executive, lay in the necessity for Parliamentary consent to the imposition of taxes. Parliament's control over government income and government expenditure is, in theory at least, the basis of its power over the Executive. But that instrument of control in its full amplitude does not belong to the Scottish Assembly. Scottish Executive income is to be determined by and granted by the UK Government subject to Parliamentary approval. Under section 45(2) the Scotland Act, the Assembly will, however, have the legal control of what may be spent by the Executive. It remains to be seen how politically effective this legal control will be. The UK precedent is not encouraging, but an effective committee system in the Assembly may work wonders. John Mackintosh (chapter 4) argues persuasively for the possible effectiveness of Assembly committees, but James Kellas (chapter 9) gives clear warning that real power may remain with the executive branch of government.

One further observation to be made is this: even in the areas in which executive, but not legislative, powers have been devolved — the 'Schedule 11' matters mentioned above — it is plain that the Assembly must have the power to scrutinize and criticise executive action. Except when a Scottish Secretary's action or inaction has been governed entirely by instructions from Westminster under the 'override' power, he is subject to the ultimate sanction of Assembly censure for what he does in exercising any of his powers.

II

So much for the constitutional interrelationship of the powers conferred on the authorities created by the Act. But what of their definition? And what of the mode of their conferment?

The Act is certainly in some matters plump and plain about it — see sections 17 and 18:

> 17(1)   Subject to section 18 of this Act, the Scottish Assembly may make laws, to be called Scottish Assembly Acts . . .
>
> 18(1)   A Scottish Assembly Act shall be law only if or to the extent that it is within the legislative competence of the Assembly . . .

Then (guided by s.18(2)) we look to Schedule 2, paragraph 1, which informs us that

> . . . a provision is within the legislative competence of the Assembly if, and only if, the matter to which it relates is a devolved matter

Section 63(2) ordains that

> in relation to the legislative competence of the Assembly, a

devolved matter is one which is included in the Groups in part I
of Schedule 10 to this Act

And then we must refer to the detailed and multifarious content of
those Groups. The main heads of devolved power being described in the
preceding chapter by Carol Craig, need not be enumerated here.

The point to be made here is as to the mode of conferment and
definition of the devolved powers — they are conferred by explicit
enumeration and defined positively by reference to fairly detailed lists of
grouped subject matters. In order to know whether the Assembly can
make a law on some matter or not, say, a new law on intestate
succession or on mental health in Scotland, one has to determine
whether the Scotland Act expressly confers legislative power over that
subject matter.

In the two cases mentioned, the Act does expressly confer power —
Group 24 of Part I of Schedule 10 includes 'Succession' as one of its
heads, and Group 1 includes 'Prevention, treatment and alleviation of
disease or illness, including . . . mental disorder'.

But that is not conclusive of the issue. For in addition to the positive
definition and conferment of power, the Act further contains a set of
express limitations which further define and delimit the power
conferred. Part II of Schedule 10 comprises 25 paragraphs which
expressly except various matters from the powers defined by Part I of
the schedule. So far as concerns the current examples, neither in
relation to mental health nor in relation to succession is there any
express exception in Part II.

Further, however, Part III of Schedule 10 lists 115 Acts of Parliament dealing with subject matters mentioned in the Groups in Part I;
Assembly legislation, it is provided, may amend, abrogate, add to or
qualify the existing law as laid down in these Acts only to the extent
that these Acts are expressed to be included in the devolved powers.

For one of our running examples, mental health, we find that in
relation to the Mental Health (Scotland) Act 1960, section 2(4), 'The
power to recommend to Her Majesty the appointment of Commis-
sioners is not included'. So the Assembly can legislate for anything
other than that. Had we been interested in the question of abortion, we
should, on the other hand, have found that the Abortion Act 1967 is
'not included', whereas in relation to kidney donations etc., the
Human Tissue Act 1961 is 'included'.

So far so good: but what about our example of intestate succession?
Since the modern law is statutory, based on the Succession (Scotland)
Act 1964 as subsequently amended, we might expect to find reference

to that Act in the columns of Part III of Schedule 10. But it is not there mentioned at all.

The necessary inference is that, since express power to legislate on succession is conferred, and since that power is nugatory unless it includes power to change the existing body of statute law, the Assembly has an unqualified power to amend the 1964 Act, and related Acts. So, effectively, Part III operates only as enunciating express exclusions of power — it seems both confusing and redundant that there are some Acts which are expressed to be 'included' at all.

In any event, these are not the only express exclusions of power stated in the Act. There are others, notably paragraphs 2-7 of Schedule 2, and section 64.

We may conclude that the conferment of legislative power on the Assembly is achieved by affirmations as qualified by a somewhat scattered and complex set of negations, and an all-encompassing general negation — whatever power is not explicitly devolved is retained.

The same, it should be added, is true of the executive powers, and subordinate legislative powers, of the Scottish Executive. As stated above, the range of executive power conferred is wider than the range of legislative powers. But the same rather complicated process of affirmation succeeded by negation characterises the conferment and definition of the devolved powers.

Thus, in relation either to the Assembly or to the Executive, anyone who wished to know whether a given matter is devolved must first discover whether it has by any provision of the Act been affirmatively included in devolved powers, then he must carefully scrutinize all the various negating provisions to check that it has not been expressly reserved. A necessary condition of that checking process will be access to the Acts of Parliament cited here and there in the Scotland Act; but that, of course, does not guarantee understanding. One fears that only lawyers and Civil Servants, but by no means all of them, will be able to work out or give reliable advice on the full meaning of the affirmations as qualified by the negations.

Beyond doubt, this complexity and difficulty of comprehension is a defect of the Act. It infringes the principle of intelligibility of law, a principle most to be prized in constitutional enactments. Citizens will have difficulty in framing a clear idea of what their Scottish level of government can do, and of what it is responsible for. This will impede exercise of the crucial right to complain — if I know what I want to complain about, I ought to know to whom to complain. Elected members of the Assembly, at least to begin with, will in many cases lack an exact appreciation of their responsibilities, their authority and their opportunities. This will conceivably tend to increase the influence of the bureaucracy, unless a conscious effort is made by Assemblymen, Secretaries and other politicians to avoid falling back too readily on bureaucratic advice as to what can and cannot be done.

Elsewhere in this book (chapter 4), it is argued that there should be a strong committee system within the Assembly. The present considerations reinforce the case for that view; Assemblymen specialising in matters of education or health or private law reform via membership of relevant committees should be able to build up an exact picture of the relevant devolved area, its potentialities and its limits. It is to be hoped that they will lose no opportunity to tell the citizen body who elect them just what they can do, cannot do, and are doing. Indeed, a useful first task for each committee would be publication in plain terms of a booklet indicating the extent and nature of Assembly and Executive responsibilities in the relevant subject area.

III

So much for the boundaries, abstractly considered — and considered only from the Scottish end of the matter. Assembly and Executive power is defined by detailed affirmations qualified by sundry specific negations and by the implicit general rule that whatever is not expressly devolved remains a responsibility of the UK Government or Parliament.

But what is the character of these boundaries from the Westminster point of view? Do they in any sense impose limits on what UK authorities can do?

In the legal sense, they impose no limit upon Parliament. What Parliament by Act has done (e.g., set up a Scottish Assembly with certain powers), Parliament can by later Act undo. Parliament can do so expressly, e.g., by passing an Act removing something, say criminal law, from the Assembly's powers, or adding something, say a taxing power, to them. Parliament can do so by necessary implication, e.g., by passing an Act on some topic of criminal law which applies to Scotland and which trenches on an area of Assembly power. (Parliament is certainly not precluded from doing so — but whether by doing so it will be deemed to have removed that matter from the Assembly's future competence is a doubtful question which the Scotland Act 1978 goes no way to answering. The present rule, that every Act of Parliament applies to Scotland, as to every part of the UK, unless there is an express exclusion, might well be reversed. If Acts of Parliament, at least those touching on devolved matters, were held not to apply to Scotland in the absence of express provision, a possible area of doubt or confusion would be eliminated. And the 'application to Scotland' clause could indicate what, for the future, would be the Assembly's power in relation to the specific subject matter.)

But although the Scotland Act 1978 does not and cannot legally limit Parliament's power of legislating for Scotland, it is probable — as Geoffrey Smith points out in chapter 7 — that, by convention, Parliament will normally abstain from legislating upon them or even discussing them. Thus does formal devolution become informal (conventional) quasi-federation.

As for the British Government, the Scotland Act does remove powers from the hand of UK ministers: 'Such of Her Majesty's executive powers as would otherwise be exercisable on behalf of Her Majesty by a Minister of the Crown shall, if they relate to devolved matters and are exercisable in or as regards Scotland, be exercisable on behalf of Her Majesty by a Scottish Secretary'. The Scotland Act legally limits (UK) ministerial power in a way in which it does not limit Parliamentary power; and the power removed from UK ministers is transferred to Scottish Secretaries.

But not unqualifiedly so. By the Scotland Act, certain highly important powers over devolved matters are reserved to or granted to 'the Secretary of State' (which means, note again, any Secretary of State, not necessarily, as the Government for the present indends, a Secretary of State for Scotland) or some other 'Minister of the Crown' (section 64(3)). These it is convenient to designate the 'override powers'. These include:

(a) the power, subject to affirmative resolution of Parliament, to withhold from Royal Assent an Assembly Bill which in his view would or might affect a reserved matter in a manner contrary to the public interest (s.38). In fact, 'Royal Assent,' is strictly inaccurate. See s.17(2) '. . . a Bill shall become a Scottish Assembly Act when it has been passed by the Assembly and approved by Her Majesty in Council.'

(b) the power to withhold from 'Royal Assent' an Assembly Bill which in his view is incompatible with 'Community (EEC) obligations or other international obligations of the UK' (s.19(2)).

(c) the power, subject, in some cases, to control by negative resolution of Parliament to give directions to Scottish Secretaries to prevent them from taking, or require them to take, executive action, on grounds equivalent to those mentioned in (a) and (b) above (s.39).

(d)   the power, subject to affirmative resolution of Parliament (with the exception as in (c) above), to revoke subordinate legislative instruments made by Scottish Secretaries, on grounds equivalent to those mentioned in (a) and (b) above (s.40).

(e)   similar powers over Assembly legislation and Executive action, exercisable to prevent substantial detriment to Orkney and Shetland (s.41).

(f)   power to give binding guidelines to Scottish Secretaries governing the exercise of the industrial and economic powers conferred by the Bill (s.52).

(g)   power (exercisable by any Minister of the Crown) to extend or subsequently to withdraw power over various matters to Scottish Secretaries (ss. 43, 69).

(h)   special power to intervene in and override the exercise of devolved powers in planning matters (s.71, sched.14).

(i)   power to set borrowing limits for Scottish Secretaries (s.52).

(j)   power to exercise any existing power over devolved matters to make subordinate legislation with a view to implementing a Community (EEC) or other international obligation of the UK. This may be done by any Minister of the Crown. (s.64(2)).

(k)   power to give guidance to a Scottish Secretary as to the amount of rate support grant required for certain local government functions. (ss. 68(2), 81 and Schedule 15).

Since UK ministers are always and necessarily answerable to Parliament for doing or not doing anything which they lawfully can do, it does appear that the scope for the convention about not discussing devolved matters in Parliament may prove narrow. The limitation of ministerial powers and the extent of their exclusive transfer to Scottish Secretaries are smaller than may appear at first sight — certainly as a matter of strict law, though common wisdom expects sparing resort to the override powers in practice. Economy of effort and of embarrassment for ministers seems to dictate such sparingness.

In effect, the boundaries upon devolved powers are, as it were, one-way boundaries. It is clear that they set an outward limit to what the Scottish Assembly and Scottish Executive can do, without conversely setting an outward limit to what the British Parliament and British ministers can do.

IV

But even one-way boundaries provoke boundary disputes, and those disputes demand adjudication. We have seen that legislative acts of the Assembly, and governmental acts of the Scottish Executive, are valid in law if and only if they constitute exercises of the affirmatively defined (affirmation subject to negation) powers to deal with devolved matters.

So what happens if a case arises where it is doubtful, disputable or disputed whether what has been done constitutes an exercise of such power, or constitutes an illegitimate trespass over the line? As a matter of fact, the Assembly or Executive can purport to, or try to, do things they have no power to do. As a matter of law, such purported or attempted acts are null and of no effect. But, like all laws (and more so than some), the Scotland Act is not unequivocally clear in its terms. There is some vagueness as to the exact edges of the powers conferred. So, sometimes, it will be disputed whether an act done is, in lawyers' Latin, *intra vires* or *ultra vires.*

The Scotland Act established adjudication machinery for settling and determining such questions. The Judicial Committee of the Privy Council is to have the last say on these questions, and there are to be two possible processes for raising such questions of *vires.*

The first process operates in relation to Scottish Assembly legislation, and takes effect prior to the final stage of legislation, that of granting approval by the Queen in Council; so-called 'pre-assent review'. The Secretary of State is charged with the duty of considering every Bill passed by the Assembly and deciding whether in his view it is not, or is only doubtfully, within the legislative competence of the Assembly. In that case he is to refer the Bill (all or part) to the Judicial Committee of the Privy Council, whose decision as to its validity or invalidity is to be final and binding for all purposes. If the Judicial Committee holds the Bill to be *intra vires*, it goes to Her Majesty in Council for approval, and if not, not.

But in a case in which the Secretary of State has not referred a Bill to the Judicial Committee, but, considering it plainly *intra vires,* has passed it on for Royal approval, subsequent events may give rise to doubt about its validity. Or, simply, a citizen aggrieved by some enacted provision may decline to accept the Secretary of State's view and wish to challenge its validity so far as it bears on his interests. For example, exercising its power in matters of civil law, the Assembly may have enacted an Act dealing with the Scots law of contract. Part III of Schedule 10 *inter alia* excludes the Consumer Credit Act 1974 from the area of devolved matters. In litigation arising out of a contract to which our hypothetical Assembly Act applies, the citizen to whom it seems disadvantageous can challenge the validity of its provisions on the ground that it illegitimately trenches upon the field of the Consumer Credit Act.

In that case the Court before which this issue is raised must give notice to the Lord Advocate and his Assembly opposite number, to enable them to join in the proceedings if they see fit; and the Court may refer the issue to the Inner House of the Court of Session (if it were a criminal case, the High Court of Justiciary), which Court decides the matter, subject to the possibility of an appeal to the Judicial Committee of the Privy Council, whose decision on such matters is final and binding for all purposes.

Just in case the UK Government should find itself having second thoughts about a Bill which has passed the Secretary of State's eagle eye and become an Act, the Lord Advocate is explicitly empowered to institute of his own motion proceedings for the determination of a devolution issue. So post-assent challenges to the *vires* of Acts will not be wholly dependent on the vagaries of private litigation. (But, regrettably, there is no expressly provided process whereby a Scottish Secretary may take the initiative to determine a disputed issue of *vires*. Probably, in a case of real dispute, he will be able to seek a declarator from the Court of Session.)

To the purpose of the present book, we are much concerned with the question how devolution can work; how, indeed, it can work well. One of the key elements in the question thus focuses upon the Courts, and particularly the Judicial Committee of the Privy Council. Since they are the final umpires upon boundary disputes, the success or failure of the whole scheme must in good measure hinge upon the skill and sensitivity which the judiciary bring to bear upon their umpiring of the boundary disputes.

At one extreme, the judges might take a large and liberal view of the provisions of the Act, within the legitimate limits of the interpretive function, ascribing to the Scottish Assembly and Executive a coherent range of powers, and exhibiting reluctance to strike down as *ultra vires* any act which is not plainly excepted or excluded from the area of power expressly conferred. At the other extreme, the judges might operate a narrow and restrictive view of the provisions of the Act, holding nothing to be within Assembly or Executive power save what on any reading of the Scotland Act must be interpreted as included in quite explicit terms by the legislation.

It has to be said that, in general, the dominant present tendency of British, more particularly English, courts has been towards a stricter or narrower interpretation of governmental powers delegated by Acts of Parliament. Especially so far as concerns ministerial powers and the powers of administrative authorities and tribunals, the courts have been stringent as to the range of discretion conferred by Acts of Parliament — consider, for example, the *Laker* and *Tameside* affairs. It has also, historically, been the case that the powers conferred on elected local authorities have more than once been interpreted in a restrictive sense; though the Tameside case may be viewed as one in which the judicial decision has fortified the discretion of the elected local authority at the expense of the minister's discretion.

In such matters, a difficult and inevitably vague line separates the issue of the *merits* of the exercise of a discretionary power from the issue as to its *extent*. Bluntly, judges exhibit a certain tendency to construe decisions which appear to them unwise or impolitic as being also *ultra vires*; it is arguable that a decision such as that in *Anisminic V. Foreign Compensations Commission* ([1969] 2 A.C. 197) exhibits this tendency.

There are therefore some grounds for apprehension that the judicial handling of devolution issues may tend towards the restrictive end of the interpretive spectrum, even as respects legislation of the Assembly. But there are also other and (one may hope) stronger indications in the other direction.

First, there is the provision made in the final paragraph (number 8) of Schedule 2 of the Scotland Act:

'Paragraph 1 above [by which the Assembly's legislative competence extends only to expressly devolved matters] does not prevent a provision from being within the legislative competence of the Assembly if it is merely incidental to or consequential on other provisions are within that competence.'

Parliament thereby instructs or, (more delicately), encourages the judiciary to look to the pith and substance of the Bill under scrutiny and see whether it regulates genuinely devolved matters. If so, minor and incidental trespass over the boundary is not to be fatal.

Secondly, the phrase 'pith and substance' reminds us, and was intentionally chosen as reminding us, of the most relevant precedents to which a Court might advert in seeking to interpret the Scotland Act. The Government of Ireland Act 1920, under which the Stormont Parliament operated in Northern Ireland, devolved legislative powers to that Parliament. Judicial interpretation of that Act proceeded along the lines that if in its 'pith and substance' a Stormont enactment dealt with devolved matters, the presence in the same enactment of merely incidental or consequential provisions trenching on reserved areas was not fatal to its validity (see especially *Gallagher v. Lynn* [1937] A.C. 863, and compare *Re a Reference Under the Government of Ireland Act 1920* [1936] A.C. 352).

Thirdly, there are differences between the technique of the Scotland Act and that of the Government of Ireland Act. We have seen that the former confers powers by explicit affirmations subject to negations. The Government of Ireland Act, on the other hand, conferred a general legislative power on Stormont, subject to express reservation of enumerated matters as remaining within the exclusive competence of the UK Parliament. In point of clarity and intelligibility, that technique is indubitably preferable to the rather muddy technique exhibited in the Scotland Act and criticised earlier in this essay. But this in no way necessitates the conclusion that the devolved powers should or will be more restrictively construed in the case of the Scottish Assembly than they were in Stormont's case.

Indeed, if one considers the partly analogous instance of federations within the Commonwealth, one finds that the Canadian Constitution (i.e., the British North America Act 1867, as amended) grants powers to the Provinces by affirmative enumeration, with a general reservation of powers to the Dominion, or 'federal' Parliament, whereas the Australian Constitution grants general powers to the states subject to express reservations of power to the Commonwealth, or 'federal' Parliament. Thus, subject to the non-equivalence of devolution and federation, the Scottish Assembly's powers are granted in a 'Canadian' way, whereas by contrast, Stormont's followed the 'Australian' model.

The significance of that for our purposes is that, on the whole, the Canadian decisions (including pre-1949 decisions by the Judicial Committee of the Privy Council) show that the Canadian model favours provincial rather than federal power, by the very operation of the 'pith and substance' doctrine as applied to an enumerated list of powers.

So the Canadian precedent suggests that, whatever else may be said for or against the power-conferring technique of the Scotland Act by comparison with the Government of Ireland Act, powers conferred by that technique are readily susceptible of benevolent and liberal judicial interpretation under the 'pith and substance' doctrine — the pith and substance of which is explicitly adopted by Parliament in paragraph 8 of Schedule 2. Moreover, whereas some commentators have held that under the Canadian system federal powers are regrettably restricted owing to the extensive construction put upon provincial powers, such an objection would not apply in our case, because of the very fact which differentiates devolution from federation. The boundaries of devolved powers are, as we saw, one-way boundaries, so that liberal interpretation of devolved power does not automatically entail restriction of central power; that is true only in a federal system where the boundaries of power are, in the main, two-way boundaries.

Finally, and most important of all, we have to recall the political principles underlying the relevant principles of public law. A restrictive judicial interpretation of ministerial and administrative powers conferred by Acts of Parliament has its justification in the view that Parliament's will ought to prevail and that the rights of citizens ought to be abridged or varied only by the express determination of the Parliament which (to put it roughly) the citizens elect. There is thus implicit reliance on the principles of democracy versus those of bureaucracy. But from that point of view, it ought not to be overlooked that the Assembly is an elected body, and thus that the wisdom of its decisions is subject to testing by democratic and political process.

As to that, not merely must Assemblymen face quadrennial elections, but also their enactments must face ministerial and Parliamentary scrutiny, on policy grounds (as distinct from *vires* grounds) under the 'override' provisions. So there is double democratic/political answerability on questions of political merits. That constitutes a strong ground for judicial caution against any mis-classification of 'issues of the merits' as 'issues of the powers'. And that, on the whole, provides a ground of principle why the judiciary ought to err, if at all, on the side of a large and liberal interpretation of the competence of the Assembly.

(Be it noted that this last argument applies distinctively to issues of the *Assembly's* competence, as against issues of *Executive* power, whether under the Scotland Act itself, or as conferred by subsequent Assembly Acts. There may well be a case for a more guarded approach to the latter, in view of some, though not all, of the principles above canvassed.)

All in all it may be hoped that a liberal approach to interpretation will prevail, especially with regard to the Assembly's competence.

V

There are two strong reasons which may be pressed in favour of the broad and liberal approach to interpretation of the Scotland Act. These reasons are a belief in the citizen's right to reasonable security in his legal expectations, and a belief in the desirability of public respect for legal and political processes.

As to the first of these, nothing could be more troublesome than if a series of Assembly Acts which had passed pre-assent scrutiny unchallenged were subsequently nullified by judicial decisions actually or apparently legalistic in the pejorative sense. Reasonable citizens act in the faith that legislation by public bodies means what it says, and is valid, and can with reasonable security form a basis for their actings. That faith once dented becomes progressively harder to restore.

As to the second, which follows from the first: a too stringent interpretation of Assembly competence may encourage a suspicion that it is always worth challenging Assembly-made law. At the lowest, this may constitute a formidable weapon in the hands of dilatory or unscrupulous defenders. It may even encourage, at an extreme, disregard for Assembly laws in the hope that their validity may be successfully challenged by nit-picking through details to find narrowly legalistic grounds for challenge.

Of course, these propositions, if accepted, do not only entail that the judiciary should tend, without leaning over backwards, to apply a presumption of validity to Assembly Acts which have passed pre-assent scrutiny. They also entail that the Scottish Executive and Members of the Assembly should govern their actings with due regard to the principles and values at stake. 'Trying it on' at the legislative level may prove a hard and expensive game, the ordinary citizen being exposed to the rough end of it.

What is most to be hoped for is a generous and liberal attitude on the part of the UK authorities, both political and judicial, mirrored by a fair-minded and responsible approach at the Scottish level. (That is not to say that a Scottish Executive might not with good reason seek to negotiate extensions of power for the Assembly; the point is that such negotiations should be kept distinct from *bona fide* exercises of the powers already conferred.) That way, the Assembly and Executive, with reasonable confidence about the extent of their powers and reasonable security from arbitrary intervention *ab extra*, could proceed to make bold, imaginative and beneficial use of the not insignificant powers they have at any given time.

It is perhaps not sufficiently appreciated to what an extent there is restructuring needed in the law of Scotland. The labours of the pre-Union Scots Parliament consummated (and outshone) by the work of the great lawyers and commentators of the late seventeenth to early nineteenth centuries endowed Scotland with a remarkably clear and coherent and principled body of common law, lucidly expounded in a fairly small number of very fine treatises. Since then, necessary reform and up-dating in the light of new circumstances, new political philosophies and new prevalent conceptions of social justice has taken place. But, without ill will, it has taken place via a legislature neither equipped nor interested to make the reforms make sense in the context of the system whose bedrock is still the old common law. Reforming legislation has been spatchcocked into the system without sufficient regard to the coherence and intelligibility of the whole.

Beyond doubt, for each reform it can well be argued that the change was worth the price paid for it in itself. But the end product is one whose jumbled character has a genuine social cost, reckonable not only in terms of the very large sums annually paid to hard-pressed lawyers for the sorting out, often in a hit-or-miss way, of citizens' problems, but also in terms of the 'unmet need' for legal services, citizens whose rights go unenforced for want of understanding and fear of legal process, problems of law which legal manpower is not available to solve even if the lawyers were able to comprehend the complexity of laws lying out of the line of normal solicitors' business — and so on.

These are not, or ought not to be, the esoteric concerns of lawyers alone. The law binds citizens, and all too often gets them in a bind. There is no aspect of civil liberty more basic (as Adam Ferguson taught) than that the citizen have a tolerable comprehension of the law, without which such rights as he has are nugatory.

There is, then, potentially a great task for the Assembly in pursuing a steady programme of clarifying, consolidating, reforming and even one day codifying the law of Scotland so far as lies within its competence.

Both as to that, and as to the general administration of legal services in Scotland (so far as they are devolved) there is a good case for assigning specific responsibility to one Scottish Secretary, in charge of the 'Ministry of Legal and Home Affairs' — see chapter 5 below, where Alick Buchanan-Smith gives the case for such a 'Ministry'. There would be available to that 'Ministry' the expertise of the Scottish Law Commission. And under the committee system as proposed by John Mackintosh, there would be a real opportunity for

Assemblymen, certainly not all lawyers, to come to grips with the problems of this area.

There are, however, special problems about law-making and law reform for a country of five million people in the modern world. Not least is the simple problem about making the laws available in readable form at reasonable cost to the public and the lawyers themselves. Unprinted laws or prohibitively expensive laws are worse than mischievous. Yet printing for a small market is very costly.

The answer to this problem may lie in exploitation of new technology. Computer-assisted printing systems exist, which can in principle simplify the processes both of drafting and, ultimately, of printing and publishing legislation (and, of course, other things besides). Such systems are already in use in some comparable juris-dictions, e.g., Manitoba. Resort to such systems in drafting and printing legislation has further exciting implications, in this way: all contemporary law is, almost inevitably, bulky and built up incrementally year by year. Thus, to keep track of it through successive amendments, judicial decisions etc., is difficult and time-consuming. But essentially that is, as the jargon has it, simply a problem of 'information retrieval'. One of the prime promises of computer technology is that it can simplify information retrieval by means of electronic data processing — provided the data exists in, or can be reduced to, machine-readable form. But if legislation is already being produced via computer technology, one part of the information retrieval problem is already attended to. There are other and tougher problems. But current work in the USA suggests they can be overcome.

Dr A.G. Donaldson at Edinburgh University is at present engaged in research under the auspices of the Scottish Legal Computer Research Trust aimed at clarifying the potentialities of 'computerisation' in relation to the Assembly's legislation, and the implications it might have for the rational designing of the Assembly's legislative process — the 'stages' of Bills etc. So there is the possibility that when — or if — the Assembly comes to regulating its own procedures by Standing Orders etc., and to providing for the printing of Bills, Acts and the like, its members will be in a position to act with foreknowledge, and to exploit rather than be exploited by the new technology — far less let its potentialities go by default.

VI

A necessary corrective to the concentration in the foregoing sections on governmental powers will be to reflect in this section on the no less vital constitutional topic of civil rights and liberties. How far is there a risk that Assembly laws or Executive actings may infringe basic rights of the citizen? Should that risk be forestalled by enactment of a Bill of Rights?

The current state of argument on a Bill of Rights in general appears in the main to favour the view that any Bill of Rights brought into operation in the UK generally or Scotland particularly should follow exactly the provisions of the European Convention for the Protection of Human Rights and Fundamental Freedoms, as the House of Lords Select Committee recently recommended, or should at least be modelled on those provisions, as for example the SNP proposes. But while there is to that extent substantial consensus on the content for a Bill of Rights *if* there is to be one, there remains disagreement whether there should be one.

It is common ground that the general record of the UK on human rights issues hitherto has not been noticeably worse than the record of other states parties to the European Convention. To that extent a Bill of Rights would not necessarily make a great difference. But it can be argued *Pro*, that any infringement of these rights is unacceptable, and that it would be preferable that remedies for such infringements be available to aggrieved parties in the British Courts rather than by cumbersome and expensive recourse to the European tribunals. *Contra*, it is argued that to do so would be to risk an excessive aggrandisement of the powers of the Courts over elected political authorities, that interpretation of the type of provisions contained in the Convention goes beyond the normal range of British judicial activity and expertise and that in any event to enact so ostensibly sweeping a measure with so little practical pay-off would be undesirable. (For a fuller and better summary of arguments see the *Report of the Select Committee on a Bill of Rights,* House of Lords Paper 176, 1978.)

So far as concerns the Scottish Assembly and Executive, there is one ground on which it might further appear unnecessary to take any affirmative action in this matter. The 'override' powers of the Secretary of State include, it will be recalled, an absolute and unreviewable power to withhold from Royal approval any Assembly Bill which in his opinion is not compatible with an international obligation of the UK, and similar provisions govern Scottish Executive actions. (See sections 19(2), 39(2), 40(2).) Since the UK is under an international obligation to conform with the European Convention, the 'override' power covers infringements of rights protected thereby.

But (a) it is in principle objectionable to leave issues of right to the sole adjudication of ministers rather than judges; and (b) the Scottish Assembly may prefer to provide other protection than that against infringement of human rights in Scotland, within the devolved areas anyway.

It appears therefore that it would at least be open to the Scottish Assembly, if a majority of its members so willed, to enact a Bill of Rights protecting citizens against any infringement of the guaranteed rights in any area of devolved administration. This would produce an interesting potential effect. For if, in case of any Assembly Bill, 'the Secretary of State is of opinion that the Bill . . . provides for matters which are or ought to be provided for by or under legislation passed by Parliament and implementing and international obligation, he shall certify to the Assembly that he is of that opinion and shall not submit the Bill to Her Majesty in Council for approval' (section 19(2)).

So if the Secretary of State were faced with a Scottish Assembly Bill of Rights, he would either have to let it go for Royal approval, or certify that it provided for matters which ought to be provided for by Act of Parliament. In which latter case, the Government would be hard put to it to justify not doing what the Government holds ought to be done, and a British Bill of Rights would be the outcome. So, for good or ill, depending on your view, an initiative by the Scottish Assembly could have far-reaching consequences.

There are other, parallel areas in which the Assembly might take initiatives which could be of wider interest. Plainly, the Official Secrets Act is not of itself a devolved matter, in the general sense that the Assembly could not repeal it *quoad* governmental secrets in non-devolved fields. But as for the conduct of government business in all the devolved fields which are within that Assembly's legislative competence, there seems to be no bar to the Assembly legislating to secure more openness of government and greater freedom of public access to governmental documents. A useful model Bill and commentary has recently been published by the Outer Circle Policy Unit, and that (for example) would be available for consideration and, subject to amendment to meet the restrictions on Assembly power, adoption if the Assembly thought fit. Even if the UK Government were tempted to activate the section 38 override power, the prospect of having to win an affirmative resolution in both Houses of Parliament on this highly sensitive issue would be a considerable deterrent.

What is more, the experiment adopted in Scotland might be carried out without the heavens falling or the engine of state grinding to a halt.

In that case there would be some evidence in favour of extension of a similar scheme to cover non-devolved powers and indeed UK Government generally.

To say that the Assembly could do such things is not to say that it would. Nor is it to offer argument that the Assembly should do them — other occasions have been and will be available for pressing such arguments. For present purposes it is enough to note that the constitutional potentialities of a Scottish Assembly are considerable, and not in any way necessarily hostile to human rights or open government. It is, after all, an experiment in democracy. If it has but the will, it will have the time, the scope, and the opportunity to be experimentally democratic.

Chapter 4

Internal Procedure and Organisation

JOHN P. MACKINTOSH

On the procedure of the Assembly will turn the balance of power between the Executive and the Assembly. If the balance is to be shifted in favour of the Assembly so that back-benchers do have some real effect on policy-making and the public are informed about the issues at stake, this would require more open government than is practised in Whitehall. Such a shift of balance should have the effect of making pressure groups deal more often and more fully with the Assembly, its committees and its members than happens at present in Westminster where pressure groups concentrate on establishing direct links with ministers and officials. Such a shift of emphasis towards the Assembly should also encourage able people to stand for the Assembly, as the work done by back-benchers would be more satisfying. If more discussion and pressure took place in the Assembly and its committees, this ought to catch the attention of the public and reduce the feeling that government is a remote, secret process.

If the style and procedure of the Assembly and its degree of control over the Executive is to be different from the situation prevailing in the House of Commons, then it is essential that this new balance of power should be written into the Standing Orders of the Assembly and the new procedures adopted from the outset. Any idea of interim procedures should be discounted, as ministers and members will soon settle in to their task, interim procedures could then become hardened, and there will always be a tendency to drift back towards the Westminster model. Changes should therefore be deliberate, precise and introduced at the very beginning of the life of the Assembly.

All over the Western world, parliaments have been losing ground to the executives or administrations. This is partly a function of time. Governments can operate on the public in numerous ways at numerous levels all the time, while a parliament can only debate one issue on the floor of the House at any one time. Secondly, traditional political issues are known to politicians and lead to debates, but governments do many things whose political effect may not be apparent when they start or even throughout the process of policy-making, and parliaments have little means of searching through the activities of government to discover issues which ought to be the subject of public debate but which are lost or submerged in detail. Thirdly, parliaments, especially the members in opposition and government back-benchers, may lack information — not just facts of which there are legion — but the crucial information about what issues are open for settlement and what alterations have been proposed. There is the greater complexity of government and the advantage this gives to the permanent officials who specialise for years on a limited area of activity. Finally, there are the inhibitions caused by the tendency for all issues debated on the floor of a representative chamber to be reduced to matters of confidence in the Government, so that it becomes hard for the majority to express dissatisfaction without defeating the Government it was elected to support.

There is a real chance that the Scottish Assembly can get over many of these problems. First, it has much more time, having only certain domestic areas of policy to debate and determine. It is the case that democratic control is more effective in legislatures which deal with smaller countries or with restricted areas of competence. Secondly, an Assembly with a proper committee structure could operate on other levels besides the major clashes on the floor of the House; and these committees, if given powers to scrutinize estimates, legislative proposals and policy-formation within departments, could or should uncover all those issues which are likely to be of concern to the Scottish electorate. These committees could be adequately staffed, and Scottish rank and file MPs given the expert assistance necessary to enable them to keep abreast of what is being done by the Civil Service. Finally, the fact that the Scottish Assembly is, for practical purposes, a fixed-term Parliament means that governments can be defeated without precipitating a general election. It is to be hoped that from the start, Scottish Governments will take a more relaxed view of defeats in the Assembly and will only resign if it is clear that they have lost the confidence of a majority in the Assembly.

The forms of procedure suggested in this chapter are designed to achieve these ends, and the most important innovations concern the establishment of an effective committee structure which would give the committees adequate powers, a permanent life (coterminous with the Assembly itself) and considerable independence from the Executive.

Committee Structure

Several forms of committee structure are possible, but it is a good rule that monitoring machinery should be organised in parallel with the organisation being monitored and this suggests one committee to watch over the work of each department of the Executive. This would mean seven departmental committees, one each for finance and manpower; development; resources; housing and local government services; education; health and social welfare; and legal and home affairs. This follows the pattern set out for the Executive in chapter 5, and it would be necessary to allow committees to set up subcommittees — the Committee on Development, for instance, may want subcommittees on the Highlands or on tourism. The question arises as to whether committees should be allowed to consider subjects which are only partially under the Assembly, but clearly the Assembly will debate and the Executive make pronouncements on such matters as Scottish industrial and economic affairs and it might even be desirable to appoint subcommittees to deal with these questions. Limitations under the review procedure of the Scotland Act apply only in legislative matters and do not restrict the capacities of these committees to deliberate and comment.

A committee would also be needed for the business and procedure of the House which will be described further below.

On the financial side, it would be best to follow the pattern in the Commons and have two committees, one on the overall expenditure of the Scottish Government, its balance and priorities. A second would be an Accounts Committee to audit the past year's expenditure.

If this was done, there would be ten permanent committees. (The words 'Standing Committees' are avoided because the Standing Committees of the House of Commons are purely legislative and are microcosms of the House. The committees proposed here would combine legislative and scrutinizing powers: they would thus combine the functions of Standing and Select Committees of the House of Commons). With an Assembly of 150 members, if eight are removed as ministers, one as a Government Whip, two as Speaker and Deputy Speaker, then each Assemblyman could serve on at least two of these permanent committees. The numbers on the committees would be fixed by Standing Orders, some already requiring more members than the average while Public Accounts and the Business Committee could be smaller with 12 or 14 members. It should then be possible for the Assembly to appoint *ad hoc* committees to deal with specific problems.

Committee Functions

Legislative: Each committee would have the power to call for evidence, to summon Civil Servants and others to give advice or information. Civil Servants working for the Assembly would be under an obligation to attend and answer, while for UK Civil Servants it would be a matter of courtesy and mutual convenience. The minister in the appropriate department, or the private member who introduced the Bill, would have the right to join the committee as a member, but without the right to vote if his help was necessary when the committee was considering that specific item of legislation.

In order to get the preliminary bargaining processes out into the open and to ensure that the public interest played a part at this stage, committees should have a prelegislative role and this could be ensured by returning to a nineteenth-century model in which the first stage was the introduction, debate and passage by the Assembly of one or more explanatory founding resolutions on which any subsequent Bill would be based.

At this stage, no Bill would be printed and the minister or private member moving the resolutions would merely have to make the case for a new item of legislation in general terms. Once the Assembly had passed the founding resolutions, they would then be considered by the appropriate committee which would hear the views of the Civil Service, of the pressure groups and of any members of the public. The proceedings of the committee could be published and, if the committee gave its overall approval, then the minister or private MP who had introduced the resolution would, by such a vote in committee, be given leave to draft a Bill.

Members of the Assembly could apply to the Government draftsman for aid in drafting Bills (or amendments). Once drafted and printed, the Bill would then go to the Business Committee to be given a place in the Assembly's timetable. Then there would be, as at Westminster, a Second Reading Debate on the principle of the measure, and for this debate, members could speak only once, but no closure motion could be accepted by the Speaker. The result would be that no member could be denied a voice in the debate on the principle of a Bill.

If it passed, a Bill would then be referred back to the same committee which had considered it at the pre-legislative stage and the Bill would be examined and voted on in detail. The Second Reading rule would apply, that no amendments could be moved which sought to alter the decision in principle taken by the Assembly at Second

Reading. Once the Bill, including all amendments and all clauses, had been voted on, it would return to the Assembly for a combined Report and Third Reading. At this stage, only members who were not on the committee could move amendments and these would be moved only on matters which had either not been considered in committee or where the committee had altered the details of the Bill. Once the Report stage was concluded, the Bill would be deemed to have passed the Assembly and become law.

Scrutiny of Policy: In addition to this legislative role, each committee would be free to examine and consider any aspect of the policy pursued or which could be pursued by its department. Scottish Civil Servants would be under an obligation to answer all questions of fact, but questions of policy could be left to ministers if Civil Servants felt reluctant to answer them. Dealings with pressure groups could not be withheld, and Civil Servants and other witnesses could only refuse to answer if the matters concerned the private affairs or personal records of individuals, or were matters where private or public firms had a case on grounds of commercial confidence. A notification would be required from the Speaker of the Assembly if any information was to be withheld by ministers or Civil Servants, saying that he considered the refusal to disclose information proper under these rules. Refusals by witnesses to answer on grounds unacceptable to the Speaker would constitute contempt of the Assembly, and the Assembly could proceed against any person committing such a contempt by a motion on the floor of the Assembly.

Also, the many *ad hoc* boards, bureaux and commissions appointed by or responsible to the Scottish Government would be grouped under each sponsoring department and made subject to scrutiny by the appropriate departmental committee, the staffs of these bodies being under the same obligation as Civil Servants to give evidence. A list would have to be published by the Executive of all patronage appointments made by the Executive which carried either a part-time or a full-time salary. Nominations to such posts would have to be placed before the appropriate permanent committee whose advice and consent would be necessary before the appointment was confirmed.

Committees could issue reports at their own discretion but it should be noted that this is the method by which advisory committees like the present House of Commons Select Committees try to get action: they ask for a government response to a list of recommendations, but this would not be necessary for committees with legislative as well as scrutinizing powers, as influence over the Civil Service would arise from the power to send for Civil Servants, conduct inquiries and return to subjects to see what changes had been made. Influence over the Government would arise from ministers' desires to keep on good terms with bodies which enjoyed such extensive pre-legislative and appointment-confirming roles.

Secondary Legislation: The committees would scrutinize and could refer to the full Assembly for debate and decision any secondary legislation made by their departments over which the committee had reservations.

Estimates: Committees would examine and comment on the estimates laid before them each year by their departments and these comments would be sent to the Expenditure Committee.

Ombudsman: As there will be a single Scottish Ombudsman covering all areas of business within the competence of the Scottish Assembly and the local authorities and *ad hoc* bodies which it sponsors, and as the Scottish Ombudsman can be approached directly by a citizen as well as by members of the Assembly, there is no need for a special committee to watch over the Ombudsman. However, he will be required to make an annual report to the Assembly and this will be received, estimates for the office will be considered, and any legislation affecting the Ombudsman will go before the Legal and Home Affairs Committee.

European Secondary Legislation: Although all matters having inter-national implications are withdrawn from the competence of the Scottish Assembly, committees could consider European Secondary Legislation affecting their areas of interest and comment in the form that 'the committee notes directive or regulation No. —— from the European Commission and urges the Executive to draw the following points to the attention of the UK minister who will be dealing with the Scottish implications of this matter when it comes before the Council of Ministers'.

Committee Composition

It is essential to give the committees a secure base which cannot be altered at will by the Executive. The Standing Orders should provide for the creation of the permanent committees at the commencement of the four years of any Assembly and these committees can have members resign at their own request, but apart from this or the vacation of a seat, no changes can be made in membership for the duration of the Assembly. The party strength on committees must be proportional to party strengths on the floor of the House except that allowance must be made for any independent members who must be permitted to serve on two committees. Appointment to each committee will be by the Business Committee, taking into account the preferences of the member, his experience, interests and seniority. Any member wishing to challenge a decision of the Business Committee can only do so by a motion on the floor of the Assembly. Committees will be free to elect their own chairman, who need not be selected from among the party majority on the committee. Chairmen will act as presiding members of the committees (as happens in Select Committees of the House of Commons) with normal voting rights and not as with chairmen of Westminster Standing Committees as Deputy Speakers with only a casting vote. The chairman will, however, have to apply the Standing Order disallowing all amendments which seek to re-open issues settled during the Second Reading Debate. In this case, the decision is his alone and can only be challenged by a motion on the floor of the Assembly.

Expenditure Committee: This Committee shall receive the reports of all the departmental committees on the estimates for their departments and will then consider the overall priorities and balance of expenditure proposed by the Executive. It will indicate its view in a Report and will pass the estimates on to the Executive. This is the prelegislative stage of the Appropriations Bill. The Bill will then be framed by the Executive, go to the Assembly for the Second Reading and then back to the Expenditure Committee for its committee stage. At this stage, the Committee will have legislative powers and will be able to pass or amend each section of the Bill.

The timetable that would be necessary would be for the departments to produce their estimates for the coming year by Christmas. These would be considered by the appropriate committees for each department by February. The Expenditure Committee would have to complete its examination of the overall priorities and the committees' comments by the end of March. The Appropriations Bill would be laid and given a Second Reading in April and the committee stage of the Bill would have to be concluded by the end of June. Interim permission to spend would be required, given by a short Bill in April which would also set up any contingency fund necessary to cover expenditure later cut in the committee stage. Supplementary estimates would go through the same procedure if and when they were needed.

The present limitation on the House of Commons, that it cannot vote for any increase of expenditure other than one proposed by a minister, will be removed and in its place will be put a requirement that changes may not be voted which produce a total of expenditure greater than that proposed by the Executive.

Accounts Committee: This Committee will audit the accounts with the aid of the staff of the Auditor General and comment on any questions of efficiency and of value for money to which it wishes to draw attention.

Business and Procedure Committee: It is important that the Government should not have total control over the business and procedure of the House. These matters should not, therefore, be determined by majority votes on the floor of the House, thus, in practice, leaving control in the hands of the party Whips. As the determination of the order of business week by week will have to take careful note of the state of business within each committee and recalling that chairmen need not be selected from the majority party in each committee, it would seem reasonable to give each committee a place on the Business Committee as well as each party. For these reasons, the Business and Procedure Committee will be chaired by the First Secretary or Prime Minister (he may nominate a deputy) and will consist of the chairmen of all the other committees and the leaders of all parties with five or more members in the Assembly or their deputies. Its tasks will be:

(a) to determine the order of business to be brought before the House,

(b) to consider any questions of procedure of membership or committees and of conflicts of jurisdiction between committees. On all these matters, it will report to the Assembly which can accept or reject its recommendations,

(c) to consider any questions relating to the staff, facilities, or internal organisation of the House. When these matters are under consideration, the Committee will be chaired by Mr Speaker,

(d) for the first meeting in any parliament, before the committees have been nominated and have met to select their chairmen, the Committee shall consist of the party leaders and any chairmen of committees of the previous Assembly who have been returned to the new Assembly,

(e) the Committee may also recommend to the Assembly the appointment of *ad hoc* committees (though this in no way restricts the right of members or ministers to move motions on this point) and any changes in the size, responsibilities or functions of the departmental committees appointed to supervise the work of the Scottish Department.

Procedure of the House

At the first meeting of the Assembly after an election, the Clerk of the House shall point to the senior Assemblyman (in terms of election and, if several have identical terms, the oldest of these) who shall rise and nominate a member to act as Speaker. Then other nominations may be made and each motion will be voted on in order till a Speaker is elected by simple majority. The Speaker will then nominate and the Assembly approve a member as Deputy Speaker.

The Speaker or his Deputy will preside over all meetings of the Assembly, chair the Business and Procedure Committee (on the occasions set out above) and represent the Assembly on formal occasions. Any comment on the conduct or rulings of Mr Speaker must be by motion on the floor of the Assembly.

The Assembly will meet four days a week, on Mondays at 2.30 p.m. and on Tuesdays, Wednesdays and Thursdays at 10 a.m. The motion for adjournment will be made each day at 6 p.m. The full Assembly will be held on Mondays, Tuesdays and Wednesdays but on Thursdays the House will not normally meet and this will be a committee day. All committee meetings will be held either on Thursdays or on times when the Assembly is not sitting, unless the Business Committee decides, in view of the state of business, to declare a Wednesday a committee day for that week. The committees will be divided into two categories, A and B, one group meeting in the mornings and the other in the afternoons so that all members can function satisfactorily as members of two committees. The Business Committee, subcommittees and *ad hoc* committees can meet an any time including days when the Assembly is in session.

As there will be no committee stages of Bills taken on the floor of the Assembly and as provision has been made for all back-benchers to have the opportunity of speaking once in Second Reading Debates, no control of time is required in these cases. But the Speaker may rule out of order any speeches which indulge in tedious repetition, and the Assembly may, by motion, place a time limit on speeches, in particular Second Readings and reported Third Reading Debates. The Assembly may also, by motion, require a committee to complete its consideration of the prelegislative or committee stages of a Bill by a certain date leaving it to the committee to apportion the time thus allotted to the various clauses of the Bill.

On Mondays and Tuesdays, Executive business will have priority, but on every second Wednesday private members' motions or Bills will have priority. Any Bill or motion supported by one hundred members will have priority over all other private business. If no private business has this degree of support, members will submit their motions and Bills to Mr Speaker, who will indicate an order in which they will be taken. If a private member's day is lost by a Wednesday being declared a committee day, this must be made good by the Government surrendering one of the days when it has priority in the following week.

On ten Mondays in the year, the Opposition party (or parties), sharing the days according to their numbers, may select a subject for debate and have priority for this purpose.

At the commencement of business on Mondays, Tuesdays and Wednesdays, there will be an hour set aside for questions. Members will rise in their places, catch the eye of Mr Speaker and ask their question. The minister responsible will reply, though a member may indicate if the question is one of general policy and he would expect a reply from the First Secretary or Prime Minister. The Prime Minister may prefer to leave the reply to a departmental minister or he may accept and answer himself. Any minister may, if detailed information is requested, beg leave to provide a written answer within three days. Members may also ask written questions on matters which are largely or wholly questions of information.

After question time, government business will be proceded with on Mondays, Tuesdays and every second Wednesday unless a member rises and seeks leave to move the adjournment of the House on a matter of great urgency. He must have the support of thirty members and must make a case that the matter is within the powers of the Assembly and is a question of urgency requiring immediate consideration by the Assembly. It is for Mr Speaker to decide whether to accept or reject such an application and he need give no reasons for reaching his decision.

The motion to adjourn at 6 p.m. can be resisted by any member provided he has given twenty-four hours notice to any minister from whom he wants a reply, and any debates on such motions must be concluded by 7.30 p.m.

There will be no individual sessions during the four-year life of a Scottish Assembly. Business which is unfinished when the Assembly rises for the summer recess will be continued in the autumn. However, each October, there will be a general debate on the Government's legislative programme for the coming nine months. In its fourth year, the Assembly will rise on the last day of July and all business not

completed then will fall. Normally (that is, subject to the provisions of
the Scotland Act), Assembly elections will take place on the third
Thursday in March.

Since the Assembly is, barring the special provisions of the Scotland
Act (Section 2, sub-section 1), a fixed-term Assembly, if a motion of no
confidence is carried and a Government resigns for this or any other
reason, such a resignation has no effect on the state of business in the
Assembly or in any committees unless, after the formation of the new
Government, previous decisions of the Assembly or of the committees
are rescinded in the normal way by votes in these bodies.

Publicity of Proceedings: There will be a verbatim report of debates in
the House and of committee proceedings, though committees may
decide to sit informally. Proceedings of the House or of its committees
may be broadcast by radio or television provided this is done in a
manner which is fair to those members and parties involved in the
broadcast proceedings and is not done in a manner likely to bring the
Assembly into contempt. Any member objecting to any broadcast on
these grounds may raise the matter on a point of order and Mr
Speaker's decision on the point is final.

Pay and Facilities of Members: Membership of other Parliaments —
the UK Parliament and the European Assembly — or of elected local
authorities in Scotland is not prohibited for members of the Scottish
Assembly. But it must be noted that one consequence of giving the
Assembly a much larger role in legislation with a pre-legislative state,
in the scrutiny of the Executive and of the many *ad hoc* boards and
agencies and in the oversight of expenditure, is that members who are
not present in Edinburgh most weeks when the Assembly is sitting will
tend to lose touch with its work. To be a member and retain another
post in the central belt of Scotland would certainly be possible. It is to
be hoped that employees of all kinds in the private and public sectors will
realise that a high calibre of Assemblymen is in the interests of the
whole country and that they will encourage employees to stand and
will either help by lightening their workload or by seconding them for
a period of years to the Assembly.

It is unsuitable that members of the Assembly should be paid less
than the Civil Servants they have to supervise and it is also undesirable
that members should have to propose and vote on changes in their own
rates of pay. In consequence, it would seem best to pay members of
Assembly the same as the Principal grade in the Civil Service and to
give them the same superannuation provisions. Ministers will be paid
at the rate of Assistant Secretaries and the First Secretary the same as

the Permanent Under-Secretary at the Scottish Office. In view of the importance of committee work as well as of constituency work, members will have free travel anywhere within Scotland (claims for car journeys, free air rail and ferry tickets) and a car allowance for journeys within their constituency. Each member may nominate a person as their secretary and this person will be paid by the Assembly the current rate, determined by Mr Speaker, for a fully qualified secretary/assistant. Each committee may hire staff not exceeding three full-time posts and these persons will be paid and superannuated at an appropriate grade, considering their experience and qualifications, to be determined by Mr Speaker. (This is apart from the Public Accounts Committee whose staff is the Comptroller and Auditor General and his office).

Continuous Review of Procedure

If the objectives set out at the beginning of this chapter are to be achieved, the procedure of the Assembly will have to be adapted from time to time either as the structure of government in Scotland alters or if some of the provisions set out here do not work in the spirit that is intended. As has been said, it is vital that the new degree of control desired for the Assembly should be established at the outset, as the best security for the continued utility of that body is a membership which has tasted and learnt to value a degree of power-sharing, of give and take between elected members and the Executive which does not exist at Westminster and which, because it has never been enjoyed by UK MPs, is very difficult for them to imagine. The Assembly must attempt to make the processes of democracy not only a reality but a reality which is perceived and appreciated by the public.

of modern government that the ordinary person or organisation who has a problem which he wishes to take to government is often bewildered as to precisely where to go. Responsibilities should be clearly defined.

Second, although the economic and industrial powers of the Assembly are much more limited than some would have wished, public attention will centre on this aspect of the Assembly's work. Indeed, the individual may judge the Assembly by what it achieves for him or her in material terms of jobs and general prosperity.

Third, people generally are becoming more and more conscious environmentally. For example, hardly any industrial development today can escape severe scrutiny, not only by those whose immediate surroundings may be affected but also by a growing number of those who are concerned generally about the effects on the quality of life of the country in which we live. And this is right. As one part of a group of islands, we have to safeguard what space we have and to husband the limited natural resources which we enjoy. This conservation of our environment must be treated as something positive, not negative.

Fourth, and arising from the previous point, there is inevitably conflict between the development of resources and their conservation. Resources such as land or water are essential for development and, for that reason, their control might be a development function. However, given the scarce nature of many of our resources, it would be a useful discipline for those who have responsibility for development to have their proposals subject to test by others who are charged with responsibility for the best utilisation of resources.

The Structure

The following structure is suggested:
> First Secretary
> Finance and Manpower
> Development
> Resources
> Housing and Local Government Services
> Education
> Health and Social Welfare
> Legal and Home Affairs

1. *First Secretary*

In departmental terms, this would embrace the Scottish Cabinet Office. It is also suggested that the First Secretary should combine his role with that of Leader of the House. Although in the modern House of Commons this is a separate function, it is significant that, till as recently as 1940, this post was normally the Prime Minister's, except of course in those Parliaments when the Prime Minister was from the House of Lords. There is advantage in making the First Secretary directly responsible for the business of the Assembly since it would perforce keep him closely in touch with the Assembly itself.

2. *Finance*

There would be responsibility for the Scottish Consilidated Fund and the Scottish Loan Fund. The main tasks would be negotiation with the UK Government of the Block Grant and allocation of priorities for expenditure within Scotland. There is advantage in these tasks being performed separately from the First Secretary. In relation to the UK Government, much of the work will be of a routine nature: however, if disagreement or conflict arises, it is better that the First Secretary's intervention be reserved specifically for such situations. The same applies in relation to negotiations between Scottish departments where the First Secretary should act as final arbiter.

As the custodian of the public purse in Scotland, it makes sense that control of the Civil Service should also lie here.

3. *Development*

The development functions of the Scottish Development Agency and of the Highlands and Islands Development Board are obvious. Included as well are transport and roads; tourism; and New Towns.

There may be some overlapping of the environmental functions of the Development Agency with the Resources Deartment. However, in so far as the Agency's activities in this direction are mainly towards the rehabilitation of land which has been used previously for development purposes, this should not conflict.

In relation to New Towns, whilst these have a housing function, the basic purpose of these towns is regarded in a development sense as an integral part of regional policy within Scotland.

4. *Resources*

This would cover land-use and development; countryside; water; pollution; erosion and flooding; marine works.

It would also include agriculture and freshwater fishing. Since almost all economic functions in relation to agriculture and fishing have been reserved to the United Kingdom, there are only left a limited number of residual functions of a resource nature which fit better alongside, for example, land-use, countryside and water rather than as development functions.

5. Housing and Local Government Services

Important as housing is to Scotland, the real functions are carried out by local government anyway. There may be arguments for a separate, specific, responsibility. However, to avoid adding to the number of departments, this function lies sensibly alongside local government functions generally, including local finance.

The Fire Service is currently under the Scottish Home and Health Department. Since its operations are performed wholly by local government, it should come into this department.

Included as well should be miscellaneous services, already operated by local government, such as liquor licensing and registration. Other minor functions like Ancient Monuments, which are of direct local as well as national interest, could also be covered.

6. Education

This is an example of a department where responsibilities hang together in a logical, recognisable way. Responsibilities would include schools and colleges, arts, libraries and museums, and recreation.

7. Health and Social Welfare

If a large Executive was envisaged, these are two functions which might be separated. But given the objective of economy of size, they can go together. Indeed, in the developing field of preventive medicine and of social medicine, there is positive merit in this.

Charities, currently a Scottish Home and Health Department responsibility, can be sensibly grouped with Social Welfare.

8. Legal and Home Affairs

Responsibilities would include: crime; treatment of offenders; courts and legal profession; civil law; tribunals and inquiries.

There have, from time to time, been arguments in favour of establishing a Department of Justice, as there is in some European countries. However, it is felt that this would be elevating the department to a status which is not justified. The Scottish tradition has been the strict separation of the Crown function of prosecution from other administrative and legislative matters in the field of law. This is maintained in the Scotland Act where prosecution is a reserved function. This has to be recognised.

Following the establishment of the Assembly, the function of the Lord Advocate will be confined to the Crown Office and to his department's servicing of the United Kingdom Government in relation to reserved matters. This means a considerable diminution in his reponsibilities. It is questioned whether there will be sufficient work for two Law Officers, the Lord Advocate and the Solicitor General. The post of Solicitor General could be transferred to the Assembly.

In any case, the Assembly will require legal advice. Responsibility for this could be combined with responsibility for the Department of Legal and Home Affairs and the individual responsible designated Solicitor General for Scotland.

Number of Ministers

In the interests of economy, the number of government departments has been kept to a minimum. This will obviously be reflected in the number of ministers, which should be kept to a minimum as well. Limiting the number of ministers also has the advantage of limiting the scope of the First Secretary's patronage within the Assembly.

Clearly, there would have to be a minister in charge of each of the departments, eight including the First Secretary. These ministers would form the Cabinet.

It will probably be necessary to have a junior minister in each department, except the First Secretary's. This can be justified on account of the range of responsibility within each department and by the desirability of spreading the workload where, for example, a department is sponsoring legislation in the Assembly. However, such additional ministers are not essential and the need or otherwise could be re-assessed when the actual involvement and workload of ministers becomes clearer. Better to start with too few and build up, than to have too many with too little work to occupy them.

There would also have to be a Chief Whip and one or two assistants to control the passage of government business in the Assembly. The Chief Whip would act as deputy to the First Secretary as Leader of the House.

Accordingly, on the basis of a junior minister for each department, the total number of ministers would be fifteen and, in addition, the Chief Whip and his assistants. If ministers in charge of departments appointed Assembly Private Secretaries, the same as Parliamentary Private Secretaries in the House of Commons, another eight members of the Assembly could be involved in the Executive.

Size of Executive in Relation to Size of Assembly

There are three major parties in Scotland: Labour, Conservative and Scottish National. Given this situation, and depending on future voting patterns, it is possible that membership of the Assembly could be divided between the parties in three roughly equal proportions. Certainly, it cannot be assumed that the party with the largest number of Assembly members will necessarily have a majority.

In these circumstances, one party might govern from a minority position with the tacit support of another party: or, two parties might come together in a formal coalition. In the former case, the number of Assembly members supporting the Executive could be as low as, say, 60 to 70, or even fewer: in the latter, it could be as high as, say, 100 to 120. Obviously, where the number of Assembly members formally supporting the Executive is low, then it is not desirable that the Executive be unnecessarily large: otherwise, they will be 'all Chiefs and no Indians'.

Furthermore, if the Assembly itself is organised on a committee basis, there will be a committee for each department and also other committees such as services, procedure, etc. Ignoring the possibility of subcommittees and assuming a chairman and deputy-chairman of each committee, there would be at least fourteen, and possibly double that number, Assembly members with responsibilities outside the Executive.

In these circumstances, the number of ministers and of committee officebearers could be in the range of at least thirty and possibly as high as fifty or sixty. The latter figures would be a relatively high proportion of the total number of Assembly members. It is important that there should be a balance between the numbers of those holding office and those who are simply back-benchers. It is impossible to specify a precise figure at which the balance is tipped one way or the other: however, when the number of those with designated responsibilities approaches half of the total number of members, it is fair to conclude that further posts should not be created.

All this confirms that, for an Assembly of 150 members, the size of the Executive should be kept small and that the number of senior ministers with full departmental responsibility should not exceed single figures.

Conclusion

The Scottish Assembly provides the opportunity to establish in Scotland a structure of government in tune with modern conditions.

That is why a slavish copy of the United Kingdom model must be avoided. Equally to be avoided is change for change's sake.

Many people throughout the United Kingdom are cynical of government and disbelieving that it serves their interests. In Scotland, we are offered the opportunity for many areas of government to build a new relationship. This challenge must be accepted positively and constructively.

Chapter 6

The Political Parties

HENRY M. DRUCKER

I

IF devolution is about democracy, then its success or failure will
depend to no small degree on the way the political parties meet the
new challenges posed to them by the creation of the Assembly. All of
the Assembly members, it is safe to assume, will be members of one or
another party. The Assembly's Executive will be made up of leaders of
at least one party. The Assembly members who are not members of
the governing party, or coalition of parties, will be — and will think of
themselves as — members of opposition parties. The Assembly
members will have promised the electors of their areas that, if elected,
they will further their party's policies. The electors of Scotland will
vote for or against individual candidates primarily because of their
party labels.

Parties are an important part of our political culture. Their activities
are scrutinized daily by the press and broadcasters and yet they remain
secretive and obscure bodies. There is no generally available description
— let alone analysis of — the organisation of the parties in Scotland.
There is even less law about the political parties. Unlike the subjects of
the other chapters of this book, the parties are not accountable to the
public for their actions, and are, if anything, more secretive and closed
to public view than the Westminster Executive. Political parties are
voluntary associations of some ambitious and determined and many
idealistic people. They are controlled by people who have spent a long
time working in and for them. These people do not take kindly to being
offered free advice by outsiders about how they should conduct themselves. This is to say that there is no effective way that the parties can
be reformed unless the people who dominate them want them
reformed. This chapter is written with that constraint in mind.

Scotland approached devolution with three major and a smattering of minor parties. The major parties are the Conservative Party, the Labour Party and the Scottish National Party. Of the minor parties, the Liberal Party is by far the most important, and has been consistently represented in Parliament from Scottish seats since the Second World War. We may also expect Scottish electors in many seats to have the choice of voting for the Communist Party, the Scottish Labour Party, and various tiny Trotskyist Party candidates. There is no National Front electoral presence in Scotland as yet. Of all the parts of the United Kingdom, Scotland has the best-developed and most elaborate multi-party political system. It has moved furthest from the mould of two-party competition.

The Scottish Assembly will, therefore, be the first battleground in Britain since the Second World War in which multi-party politics will be the rule. Since a good many of the conventions of British politics are based, more or less explicitly, on the assumption of two-party competition, the Scottish Assembly, released from the bounds of that kind of fight, will inevitably break new ground. It is not too much to suggest that this factor will contribute much to making the Scottish Assembly different from Westminster. In the Assembly the various parties will have to develop new ways of marshalling their electoral support, their social support, and of making policy.

Before moving on to consider how the individual parties may handle these new problems, a caveat should be entered: a possible change concerns the electoral system. The Scotland Act provides for the use in Scotland of the so-called 'first past the post' system. It also reserves electoral law, and hence the right to change this system, to West-minster. Many people in both Houses of Parliament — including, at one point, a majority of the House of Lords — prefer some form of proportional representation. Given that there are a large number of possible forms of proportional representation which might be adopted, each of which would have different political consequences, it would be unfruitful here to take sides in the argument for or against a change in the electoral system. Nevertheless, it must be noted that Scotland will be operating a 'first past the post' electoral system with three major parties. This will produce highly unstable politics. A slight shift of votes (if felt evenly across the whole country) could produce considerable changes in the number of seats held by each of the parties. Dramatic shifts in the numbers of seats held by the major parties would be much less likely under most forms of proportional representation.

The argument for the present system is that it ensures that each party has a chance to rule and a chance to recharge its batteries in opposition. The argument for proportional representation is that it produces a legislative chamber which nearly matches the party preferences of the electorate. A system of proportional represention would also be more stable — it would produce long periods of continuity of policy. It would also make it less likely that a sizeable minority of the electorate could capture the control of government for a definite policy which was strongly opposed by the rest of the electorate. In other words, the chance that an extreme Socialist or Nationalist government could gain control is reduced under proportional representation. Given that one Scottish Party — the SNP — is committed to such a definite policy — independence — it is remarkable that the British parties have not agreed to a system of PR for the Assembly.

For the lack of any more real or manifestly superior alternative, however, I will assume in the rest of this paper that the present parties — in roughly their present strengths — and the present electoral system are in operation. Given that the present electoral system benefits the major parties and squeezes out the minor ones, I will concentrate on the major parties.

II

Devolution will face the parties with a number of issues. Amongst the most important are:

1. *Relationship between the 'British' and the 'Scottish' part of each party:*

This relationship has two aspects: the relationship between the Westminster and Assembly groups of MPs and Assemblymen and the relationship between the machines in the country which serve to get out the vote on behalf of their party for each elected group. A number of factors will affect the relationship of the two groups in each party. One is the Constitution. The Assembly will be tied to Westminster for its finance. Each party will want to persuade the Scottish electorate that it alone will bring the largest possible amount of Block Grant to the Assembly. The positions of the various parties in this regard differ. It will be possible for the Conservative and Labour Parties to claim that, if they are returned with a majority of seats — or are the major coalition partner in a future Westminster Government, then Scotland will get a large share from them. Labour's claim in this respect is likely to be slightly more credible than the Conservative's, since, on present voting patterns, Labour is the only party likely to be able to control both Westminster and the Assembly alone. Also, the Conservatives, as a predominantly Southern-English party, will have difficulty in saying convincingly that they will bring increased resources to Scotland. The Scottish National Party's position is different. They will have the easiest time saying that they would like to increase the Block Grant, but the hardest time doing anything about it. The SNP cannot hope to form a majority administration in Westminster. It might hope, however, to be a coalition partner at Westminster and to make a high level of Block Grant to the Assembly its price for supporting the larger coalition partner. The willingness of any Westminster Government to raise the level of Block Grant to the Assembly by more than purely 'economic' of 'expenditure' considerations dictate, will be increased if 'its' Scottish party controls the Assembly. The same considerations which apply to Block Grant negotiations will, we may presume, apply to such questions as whether or not the Secretary of State should use his powers to their legal extent, or whether or not Westminster should legislate further devolutions of power.

Foreign experience is not terribly helpful here, except in one respect: Canadian parties do not necessarily contest elections at all levels. The *parti Quebecuois* contests provincial elections but not federal ones. The Scottish National Party might be tempted to do the same. There are arguments for and against such a posture. On the one hand, such a policy would guarantee the purity of the Scottish National Party from the taint of Westminster compromises. This policy might also be used to rationalise the position if either the SNP finds it impossible to attract sufficiently strong Parliamentary candidates, or gets a derisory vote in Parliamentary elections, or its Assembly group is sufficiently predominate in the party to prevent what it may see as the building of an alternative and threatening power-base. On the other hand, a policy of not contesting Westminster seats would remove one potential level of power from the hands of the party (its role in any coalition, and its ability to use Westminster as a focus for publicity). Further, a decision not to contest Scottish seats at Westminster elections would leave the other parties free to contest for the loyalty of SNP voters. (The Conservative Party in Scotland decided to enter local politics since Conservatives thought its absence was weakening the loyalty of its voters in just this way. On the other hand, the Canadian parties do not seem to be over-worried by this problem.) I am going to assume, in this paper, that the Conservative, Labour and Scottish National Parties will feel compelled to contest both Parliamentary and Assembly elections in all seats in Scotland.

The relationship between the various levels of the parties is bound to be affected by the reactions of the electorate. If more people vote in Parliamentary elections than Assembly elections; more, if people vote in Assembly elections on the basis of their reaction to the Parliamentary performance of the various parties, the authority of the Assembly and the Assembly levels of the parties will be reduced. There can be little doubt that these two factors — relative levels of turnout and the independence of voting at the various levels — is an extremely important part of the continuing weakness of local government. If more people would vote for their councillors, and/or, if fewer people voted in local elections in a way calculated to reward or punish the Parliamentary government, this would be an immense boon to local government. Nothing so weakens a democratically elected body than the recognition that it is a residual category in the minds of the electors. Assembly members and Assembly executives will have to strive hard to prevent their level of government becoming a residual category. Assembly members and executives of the Scottish National and Labour Parties have the most at stake here. The Scottish National Party needs the Assembly to succeed for ideological reasons; Labour needs it to succeed because Labour created the Assembly.

This brings us to the relationship between the machines of the two parties. There are a number of alternatives. The parties may develop unified machines which will contest all elections in their areas: they may develop separate machines for the two levels; one or another party may have separate machines while the other parties remain unified; or they may fudge the question. The simplest alternative and the one which I think we can assume that all the parties will adopt from the beginning is to have a unified machine. Individuals will join the party and work for it in all its elections. The formal and informal rules of the parties will have to be changed slightly to accommodate the new selection of Assembly candidates and the election of Assembly members. But if this alternative is adopted it is not difficult to see that tensions will arise within the unified structure.

These tensions will not make it easier for Assembly members and Westminster MPs of the same party to co-operate in handling complaints from constituents. It will not be a healthy thing for the Assembly if Assembly members and MPs do not co-operate over citizens' complaints. Not simply the devolution settlement, but the whole democratic process will lose respect — and citizens' complaints will not be attended to. Given that functions are shared out between the various levels of government in such a haphazard way, and that existing politicians find it difficult to co-operate, it seems hopeless to propose rules for co-operation. But both sides ought to pass on complaints from citizens and not wilfully complicate the citizen's attempts to gain redress of his grievances.

2. *Solidity of Party Support:*

The potential conflict between the Westminster and Edinburgh part of the parties is well known both within and outside the parties. Less appreciated is the potential for conflict within the parties on sub-Scottish divisions. The Labour and Conservative Parties are not backward at claiming that the Scottish National Party is an unnatural coalition of the forces which will have great difficulty remaining within one party once it has to take a definite stance on social and economic issues. Such conflicts may well emerge within the older parties as well. There are obvious conflicts of interest on Assembly topics between rural and urban interests. If the Assembly chooses to spend relatively more money on rural schools than the present Government does, it will have to find the money to pay for this in some urban policy. Similarly, a policy on rural land acquisition might be very popular with agrarian socialists, but will have little charm to city slum dwellers. Conversely, a policy to develop the East End of Glasgow has little attraction for Borderers. The Labour and Conservative Parties with their strongly delineated geographical bases will be tempted to take one or another side on this issue. But if one area — say Glasgow — is thought to threaten the interests of all the others, a coalition against it which cuts across existing party lines is not difficult to envisage.

Divisions of the support of the parties could also occur on sectarian lines. If the Executive, in a fit of euphoria in the first years of its operation, embarks on a programme of liberalising social policies, an unholy (or, all too holy) alliance of Catholics and Presbyterians could emerge to thwart it. The parties would have real difficulty in coping with such an alliance.

The concentration of Scotland's Catholics (16% of Scots are Catholics) in the Strathclyde Region (one-third of Strathclyde citizens are Catholics), and the further concentrations of Catholics in the Labour Party (the most recent poll (March 1978) showed that 75% of Scottish Catholics favoured Labour) opens up the real possibility of the divisions on regional and sectarian lines reinforcing one another. The Labour Party Assembly group is likely to be dominated by its Strathclyde contingent. The other parties are likely to be weak in Strathclyde. This could put pressure both on Labour's non-Strathclyde members and the Strathclyde members of the other parties. It could also lead to the emergence of hitherto unexpected coalitions.

The system of committees (proposed in chapter 4) will provide a convenient focus for any anti-Executive coalitions which may emerge. If, say, an SNP-dominated Executive proposed to restrict the expenditure of public money paid to sectarian schools, the Assembly Committee on Education might be the scene for the emergence of an unusual coalition of members. But would the Conservative and Labour Parties endorse such a move officially? And how would the SNP deal with those of its members who participated? More — how would the electorate deal with parties which had seen to be divided on a whole series of social issues in the previous Assembly? Problems of this kind might encourage the breakup of all the present large parties. The fact that the Executive would not have to call an election if it lost a few important votes in the Assembly would also remove one of the factors which has operated in the past to keep the parties together — the need to keep their party in office and the other side out.

3.   Control of Assembly Group:

In the ideology of the Labour Party, control of the elected members of the party, by the party, is an important issue. It is not difficult to see why this should be so, and though never formally adopting this ideology, the other parties are moved by it. Unless the party exercises some control over the members who get elected under its label to the Parliament or Assembly, it is hard to believe that the party is a democratic organisation at all. Of course, nowhere, and certainly not in the Labour Party, has such control ever been satisfactorily exercised: too many things work against it. There is, perhaps most important of all, the ambition and pride of the elected members. There is also the fact that the Assembly or Parliamentary groups of a party have to respond quickly to changing events which the party cannot keep up with. There is also the feeling in the party of many elected members that they know better than the party does what the electorate wants, and that even if they act solely out of electoral considerations, the party ought to allow the MPs or Assembly members as much manoeuvrability as possible.

The problems which political parties have had in controlling their elected representatives in town councils and Parliament will be magnified in the Assembly. Whatever else happens to made the Assembly like Westminster, in this respect it will be quite different. This is true for two quite unrelated reasons. In the first place there is the multi-party system. This will make it more than likely that some Assembly Executives are coalitions from time to time. Control of one's own party when that party is forced to make private bargains with another party to remain in power, is all but impossible.

The other feature of the Assembly which will make party control of the Assembly group untenable is the committee system (see chapter 4). The committees and their chairpersonships will be sources of power and influence. The people who hold these posts will not readily take dictation from the central office of their party — particularly if they have a safe seat and a compliant local organisation. Moreover, the committees' job will be to criticise the Executive. They will behave much as the Committees of the American Congress. Senator Fulbright was not beholden to the Democratic machine — and rarely to a Democratic president. A similar situation may quickly evolve in Edinburgh. The proposals for a committee structure go a long way towards abolishing the Government-Opposition confrontation. Certainly members of the Assembly whose parties are not part of the Executive may have, in the committee system, an alternative source of power which will make them much less susceptible to party control than leaders of the Westminster opposition possess.

The struggle for the control of the Assembly groups of the various parties will take on different forms in the case of each of the parties. The Conservative Party retains enough of its old form as a Parliamentary caucus controlled by its leader, for the fight for the control of that party's Assembly group to take the form of a battle between the Conservative leader of the day and the leader of the Conservative Assembly group. Partly because that party is committed to campaigning for a 'no' vote in the devolution Referendum, it is unwilling to prepare for the Assembly — such preparations would be tantamount to an admission that it will lose the Referendum. It is possible the Conservative leader will nominate a leader of the Assembly group from amongst the successful Conservative candidates for Assembly seats. Alternatively it is possible that some formal consultation, or even election from amongst the Assembly members who are Conservatives will take place. It is unlikely that ambitious Conservative Assembly members will wish to do anything which will antagonise their Parliamentary leader. If the leader of the Assembly group is nominated by the party's Westminster leader — whether with consultations or not — it will be difficult for the leader thus elected to exercise much independence *vis a vis* his party's Westminster leadership. In that case, the Conservative Party will have lost an opportunity to establish itself as a genuinely Scottish party.

The Labour Party, on the other hand, is committed to campaigning for a 'yes' vote in the Referendum and is already beginning to debate the issue of control of the Assembly group. At the 1978 Annual Conference of the SCLP, the party passed a document, *Towards a Manifesto*, which committed the party to holding Labour Assembly members accountable to the party: 'there is a growing mood in the party that those who are elected as Labour representatives should be accountable to those who selected them, as well as the electorate in general'. *Towards a Manifesto* went on to assert that 'both the electorate and the Labour movement have a right to expect the implementation of that programme. We will examine ways in which the functioning of the Labour group in the Assembly can be organised on a more democratic basis'. There are various ways in which that democratic basis might be established.

The local government model might be followed. The Executive of the SCLP could put one or more of its members onto the Assembly group — or its Executive. This would at least keep the group and any Assembly Executive in touch with the party and let the party Executive know what is going on. (The party is already committed to reserving two places on its Executive for two Assembly members.) Such a procedure need not threaten the Labour Assembly group with party domination since the non-Assembly members would be few. Other more dramatic proposals would go further in the direction of democracy, but would almost certainly be unacceptable to the Assembly group and might even be unworkable: it would be possible, for example, for the entire Scottish Council Executive to meet in joint session with the Assembly group. There is little sense in proposing such reforms, however. There would be no support for them amongst the Assembly group and even if formally enacted could easily be circumvented. (It would be useful for a Labour-dominated Assembly Executive, for example, to see the Labour group hobbled by rigid and unworkable democratic forms, because this would discredit the group and make it easier for the Assembly Executive to go its own way.)

The problems of control of the Assembly group will be complicated for both the British parties in a way which will not trouble the SNP. For the British parties, any innovation will be carefully scrutinized to see that it does not create so attractive a precedent that the Westminster group of the party is obliged to adopt the Scottish procedure. Even though the Labour Party's Scottish Council is formally free to make policy for the party's Assembly group, it will not want to antagonise Transport House. The SNP will be largely free from this sort of problem. Otherwise, the considerations relating to the party control of the Assembly group which relate to the Labour Party will weigh on the SNP.

Party control of the Assembly group will, however, raise a dilemma for the Scottish National Party which will also be noticeable for that party in a number of other areas. It will be tempted to have the newest and best procedure in each aspect of the Assembly business. Unencumbered by strong Westminster attachments or a history of past compromises, it will be relatively easy for the leaders of the Scottish National Party to choose procedures which reflect the most up-to-date ideas. But the Scottish National Party will always be slightly wary of becoming too comfortable in the Assembly or too proud of the way it works the Assembly's procedures. On the one hand, it will be tempted to show that the new procedures are unworkable, and to create friction with Westminster to this end. Such trouble will tend to justify its argument that the present devolution of power is insufficient to Scotland's needs. The SNP leaders will also be tempted to seek out sources of conflict because fights with Westminster will make sure newspaper copy, and because many of the SNP's supporters will be anxious to see their party leaders fighting the English. But, on the other hand, the SNP has an especial interest in convincing the Scottish people and the British Government that devolution is a success. Only in that way will the former support or the latter allow any further devolution of power. The question of party control of Assembly members will raise the issue.

4. *Choice of Leader:*

The Conservative Party has yet to begin to consider how it will select its leader. I have suggested that two ways are possible: the leader of the Assembly group could be chosen by the British leader (currently Mrs Thatcher) or the leader could be chosen by the Conservative Assembly group.

The Labour Party is currently arguing within itself about its procedure for selecting its Parliamentary leader. This debate is reflected in its internal discussions about its choice of Assembly leader. It will be tempting for the party to allow its Assembly group to choose its own leader. This would follow the analogy of Westminster. It would also avoid the embarrassment which would result if the leader were chosen before the election by some other body — say the Executive of the SCLP — in which case the leader might not even be elected to the Assembly. On the other hand, the first Assembly campaign will be attended by an intense blaze of publicity and unless there is a leader-

designate, the press will choose its own leaders and they will make
conflicting statements.

Various proposals for a selection procedure have been aired. The
leader could be chosen by the Assembly group whether or not that
group is topped up by some SCLP Executive members. The leader
could be chosen by the SCLP Executive. He could be chosen by a joint
meeting of the two bodies, or by a specially called Conference.

The Scottish National Party might well want to take advantage of
the opportunity of selecting the leader of its Assembly group to
demonstrate that it is a more democratic party than the older parties.
Certainly, there will be no equivalent in it to the counsel which both
Labour and Conservative Parties will hear from those who are used to
choosing a leader from amongst the Parliamentary group. The options
open to the Scottish National Party are like those open to the Labour
Party, with two exceptions. The Scottish National Party might want to
have its Assembly leader chosen by a Special Meeting of its National
Council. It will also labour under the difficulty that it has very few safe
seats, and will thus not be able to place its leaders in safe seats — or
even in seats it has confidence it might win. Both Labour and
Conservative have safe seats in fair number, thus they will know once
their candidates are selected who many of the Assembly members will
be. The Scottish National Party will only know that if the electoral tide
is in its favour it will have a large number of members; and if the tide
is against it, it might have very few. It will thus be impossible for the
Scottish National Party to choose its leader with any confidence before
the first Assembly election.

5. *Role of Paid Agents:*

One obvious source of conflict within the parties is over the time and
loyalty of full-time agents. The position differs in the three major
parties. The difficulty is most relevant to the Conservative Party as it
has the largest number of full-time agents. There are twenty-one paid,
full-time, qualified agents in Scottish Conservative Constituency
Associations. In addition, eight Associations have a full-time
Organising Secretary (the difference between the two jobs is not clear
to people in the party — agents, however, have a formal qualification
and a higher salary). The agents are chosen by the Constituency
Associations. Some of these agents are already conscious that the
party's decision in the mid-sixties to contest local elections has put a
considerable strain on their time. The need to further contest
Assembly seats might strain their resources even more. It is almost
difficult not to believe that there will be conflict between Conservative

MPs and Assembly members for the time of the agent. It may be very tempting for local Constituency Associations to appoint Assembly agents to avoid this conflict — but raising money for such people would cause a problem.

From the second Assembly election on, the Parliamentary seats will be divided into two or three Assembly seats. It is possible that some present Conservative Parliamentary seats will be divided into a safe-ish Conservative Assembly seat and a seat which will be won either by Labour or the SNP. A rational use of resources would dictate that the party put its greatest energy into trying to win the other party's seat. But the balance of strength within the Constituency Association will be in the Conservative Assembly seat. The agent will be right in the middle of this argument.

The Labour Party has six full-time paid Constituency agents in Scotland and is appointing a seventh. Labour's agents are appointed by those who pay them. Thus, two Dundee agents and the new agent for Glasgow will be appointed directly by Transport House in London. The agent in Edinburgh is appointed jointly by Transport House and by the Edinburgh District Party. The other agents are appointed by their local Constituency parties. Because it has fewer agents than the Conservative Party, the problem of the conflict between these officials and potential conflict for the time and loyalty of these agents, is of less importance for the party as a whole. (In seats where there is no paid agent, the MP or the Parliamentary candidate chooses his own agent with, if he has any sense, the advice of his Constituency party.) However, the Labour Party's two nationally appointed agents and the one jointly appointed agent, will raise more thorny problems for the party. To whom will these people be responsible when there are conflicting demands on their time? Presumably to the MP and not the Assembly member or candidate.

The Scottish National Party does not have this problem. It does not have paid Constituency agents. Some of its MPs and parties have Secretaries — but this should not lead to any difficulties.

It is perhaps worth noting here that, while the Labour Party is virtually unanimous in regretting the small number of its paid agents, the Conservative Party is not unanimous in its praise of paid agents. There are some people within the Conservative Party who believe that agents are too expensive (salary range is now £3,500 to £6,500 and some have a car and expenses as well), that they simply serve to give volunteers an excuse not to work for the party, and that in some cases, the agent has too much power within the Constituency Association.

This anti-agent element in the Conservative Party may be strengthened by conflicts over the agent's loyalty between Parliamentary and Assembly electioneering.

6.   *The Role of Central Offices and Finance:*

All the major parties' central offices are hard pushed to do their jobs with the resources available to them. During Parliamentary by-elections and general elections they are stretched beyond their maximum. The need to organise Assembly elections, write Assembly manifestoes and fight Assembly by-elections, in addition to their present work, will present each with problems which cannot possible be solved with the present level of finance. Each party will need more paid staff.

Conservative Constituency Associations are not branches of the national party. They are autonomous associations which affiliate to the national party, the Scottish Conservative and Unionist Association (SCUA). On the whole, the autonomy of the local associations is greater in Scotland than it is in England and is particularly noticeable in the rural areas of Scotland — i.e., in the areas from which the party draws most of its votes. The party has periodically re-organised its Constituency Associations into areas. The purposes of these re-organisations is to encourage the stronger to help the weaker. It has rarely worked. The areas were established in 1965. Each was to have an agent appointed by the chairman of the Scottish Conservative Party. Suspicion from the Constituency Associations was one reason why this scheme failed. The number of area agents was reduced in 1968, in 1970, and the idea was given up altogether in 1975.

SCUA is the public face of the Conservative Party in Scotland. It is not a strong body. The President of SCUA changed each year until 1977, when the period of office was made two years. One reason for the weakness of the SCUA is the existence of a parallel organisation — the Central Office. The Scottish Conservative and Unionist Central Office (SCUCO) grew out of the Chairman's Office of the Unionist Party of the pre-mass politics era. The Chairman of SCUCO is appointed directly by the Leader of the Party. The greater authority of the SCUCO over the SCUA is seen in the comparison of this method of appointment with that of the President of SCUA. The latter 'emerges' from the ranks of the Constituency Associations.

One reason for recent reforms in the Conservative Party organisation was finance. The Scottish Conservative Party has simply never enjoyed the kind of support from Scottish industrialists and businessmen which the British Conservative Party has. From 1965-75 the Scottish Central Office was virtually supported by two men — Lord Fraser and Hugh

Stenhouse and their personal friends. In 1970, for example, the party raised £118,350. Of this the party Treasurer's firm alone gave £25,000. This sum contrasts vividly with the £8,744 which was raised in that year by the Constituency quota scheme. The obvious way to continue to support a reasonably healthy full-time organisation in Scotland was to get London to pay for it.

If I am right to suggest that the coming of the Assembly will demand more resources from the parties, then this will have the para-doxical result in the Conservative Party of depriving that party of even more autonomy as it will be forced to depend to an even greater extent on London money.

The Labour Party in Scotland operates under similar, if less obvious, constraints. It has five full-time political officials in Scotland, all of whom are paid for and chosen by Transport House. The Labour Party has already decided that its Central Office will work both to the party's Assembly group and for the election of Labour MPs in Scotland. Where the Conservative Party in Scotland has two parallel organisations which are sometimes in conflict, the Labour Party has one organisation (SCLP) which is controlled by an Executive which is elected by the Constituency parties and the trades unions at the party's annual conference. But this organisation is officered by officials paid by London. Divisions within the Labour Party in Scotland — of which there are a number — are rarely along 'SCLP versus officials' lines.

Constituency parties and trade unions affiliate to the British Labour Party in London. They pay the Scottish Council a small affiliation fee on top of their affiliation fees to London. In 1977 Scottish Council had an income of £4,222.67 from this source. This is not a large sum. Labour has a problem similar to the Conservatives. As capital has gone to London, so have the unions. The once autonomous large Scottish unions who are affiliated to the TUC have been merged with their British counterparts — this leaves no independent base for financing a Scottish Council of the Labour Party. Thus the same paradox — devolution to an Edinburgh Assembly will mean evolution to the British party — affects Labour as affects Conservative parties. The Labour Party does have one advantage in this respect which the Conservative Party lacks. The British Labour Party knows that it has traditionally won a high proportion of the Scottish Parliamentary seats. It will thus remain fairly easy for the SCLP to argue for more than its present share of resources on the grounds that the party gains much from the large number of Scottish MPs.

The Scottish National Party is served by ten full-time and three part-time staff in Edinburgh. They are all paid by the party in Scotland. There can be little doubt that the primary focus on their interest after devolution will be the Assembly group of their party. This clear-cut direction will be of obvious advantage to the party in the Assembly (though it may make the lives of the SNP MPs even more isolated than they already are).

There is bound to be pressure from within the Assembly for the appointment from public funds of further assistants to the various parties. They will want Research Officers for the party groups — they may want paid Whips offices too. Such additional assistance will go some way to helping the parties (particularly those not part of the Executive) to control the Executive. As such, it will strengthen the democracy of the Assembly and make it compare favourably with Westminster. It is likely, however, that the appointment of such additional officials will affect the balance of power within the parties. It will aid the Assembly groups at the expense of the Westminster groups of the parties. If there are any large number of such paid officials they could (in the Conservative and Labour Parties particularly), outnumber the party officials paid for by London. This public money would help to counteract the influence of London money on the control of the British parties' Scottish sections. In such a situation we might even expect some pressure for greater autonomy for the Scottish parts of the British parties.

7.   Choice of Candidates:

Each party will be affected by its expectation of ruling the various tiers of government. Conservatives will have a much better chance of being part of a government team at Westminster than in Edinburgh. The position for the Scottish National Party is reversed. In each case potential candidates will be — and not dishonourably — attracted to the political forum which their party has the best chance of controlling. Thus, the Conservative Party's best men will continue to go to Westminster, while the Scottish National Party's best people will gravitate to Edinburgh. The Labour Party, which might conceivably control either legislature, will presumably find that some of its best men go to one legislature, the rest to the other.

The Labour Party has already decided to exclude 'dual-membership' of the Assembly and Westminster for its nominees after the second election for the Assembly. The other parties may well follow suit. Whether they do or not, the addition of another tier of elected government, whose elections will not coincide with elections for any of the existing tiers, will increase the likelihood of by-elections. If an Assembly member wins a Parliamentary seat he may resign his Assembly seat. Similarly, a newly elected Assembly member might resign his Regional or District Council seat. This is an additional reason for the re-organisation of local government by the Assembly after devolution.

8. *Policy Formation:*

Parties do not make policy at Party Conferences. Each, in its different way, makes policy in private. Largely because the television networks decided to broadcast first the British and subsequently the Scottish Conferences of the parties, an expectation has grown up that the parties are making their policies at these meetings. Both the Labour and Scottish National Parties give credence to the notion that they make policy at their Conferences in their Constitutions. The Standing Orders of the SCLP states: 'The Scottish Council Annual Conference shall decide from time to time what specific proposals of legislative, financial or administrative reform shall be included in the Party Programme.' The Constitution and Rules of the SNP states unambiguously: 'The Annual National Conference of the Party shall be the supreme governing body of the Party.' The Conservative Party makes no such claims for the Annual Conference of SCUA. The most the current President of SCUA would claim is that the aim of the Conference is . . . 'to enable as many of the Conservative membership as possible to express their view and, in addition, the Conference particularly is a platform for those who are in charge of political briefs within the Party to express their opinions in response to the debates'.

The Annual Conference of SCUA (in May) is not a delegate meeting: it does not make policy. In practice, Constituency Associations can send as many representatives as they choose. Conference meets on Thursday, Friday and Saturday — a fact which helps to account for the predominance at Conference of women and older people. (Motions in 1969, 1971 and 1977 urging the party to meet as the others do, over the weekend, have not been taken up.) Motions for debate are chosen by the Conference Agenda Subcommittee of the SCUA Executive. Conference's weakness as a policy-making body is indicated by the voting method which is by show of hands. If a ballot vote is decided upon, then members use the ballot papers in the Conference handbook, a handbook which is issued to all attending, including members of the public, political scientists and the press. The Conference may influence the leadership but never bind it; ballots are at the discretion of the chairman.

Both Labour and the SNP have more elaborate, apparently more democratic procedures than the Conservative Party. It is difficult to believe that an openly undemocratic procedure as that now employed by the Conservative Party will suffice for a policy-making machinery after devolution. The Conservative Party leadership is already under some pressure from within its party to involve individual party members in the making of policy. Some steps in this direction have been taken with the establishment of various policy committees by SCUA.

The Labour Party was formed by trade union and socialist groups outside of Parliament. In theory it has an elaborately democratic decision-making machinery. Each Constituency party and affiliated trade union is allowed to send in two motions for Scottish Conference (which meets in March) each year. Previously, motions had to relate to Scottish topics; this is no longer the case. The motions are grouped by subject by the Executive and circulated. Each Constituency party and affiliated union may then propose one amendment to a motion. Every party has a strictly limited number of delegates (usually two — but sometimes more) and each trade union has a number of delegates to Scottish Conference which reflects its number of affiliated members. Some unions affiliate on the basis of more members than they actually have — this is a way of getting more votes and paying higher dues to the party. At meetings of delegates on the eve of Conference, motions on the various subjects are 'composited' into massive — sometimes contradictory — resolutions. Conference then debates and votes on each subject on which there is a resolution.

The Executive can usually control the debate. It has the right of reply after each debate and its reply is of ten minutes where the other contributions are strictly limited to three minutes each. It ought to be able to mobilise the support of the major trade unions with their large block votes for its position since the Executive is dominated by these unions in the first place. In practice, the unions do not like being dictated to by the Executive, and different unions vote on different sides of most questions. It is difficult, however, to dignify the proceedings with the description 'debate'. In the 1978 Conference the delegates voted in two and half days for policy on Housing, Local Government, Scottish Assembly, Party Organisation, Industry and Employment, Industrial Democracy, Economic Policy, Public Ownership, Transport, Old People's Charter, Health and Social Security, Land, Open Government, Law, Education, EEC, Fuel and Power, Rural Affairs, Taxation, Public Enquiries, and Single Parent Families. The debate on

Housing lasted forty minutes; on Education the Conference spent thirty minutes. In the later 'debate' not one speaker mentioned the Pack, Munn or Dunning Reports — three crucial reports about the future of education in Scotland which had been published in the previous year.

The most dispiriting thing for the Assembly's good government is the delegates' preferences for debate on subjects — Public Ownership, for example — over which the Assembly will have no control. Labour needs to reform this procedure. At very least one day of the Conference ought to be set aside for debate on Assembly topics. The 1977 revision of the Rule and Standing Orders of the SCLP did not specify any particular time for debate on Assembly subjects.

The procedures of the Conservative and Labour Parties represent two ends of a spectrum. The Conservative Party hardly bothers to pretend that its policy-making procedure is democratic. It certainly does not claim that its Conference makes its policy. There is a perfectly reasonably defence of the Conservative position: no body of 1,000 people meeting once a year could possibly make sensible policy across the whole range of social issues. The Labour Party, in direct contrast, claims that this is a perfectly good defence of this procedure: policy should be made by the party, not its leadership. The procedures adopted by the Scottish National Party go some way to avoiding the difficulties of the older parties.

Scottish National Party policy is made, in theory, by its Annual Conference. The Conference meets for three days each May. It consists of two delegates from each branch of less than fifty members (with one additional delegate for each additional fifty members), and one delegate from each Constituency Association. (It is interesting to note that the SNP Conference is dominated by the branches, not the Constituencies Associations — Labour is organised the other way round.) But the major difference between the SNP's Conference and Labour's Conference is that SNP policy has been digested and discussed by the party at two other national bodies before it reaches Conference. These bodies are National Assembly and National Council. National Council meets at least four times a year and is composed of a smaller number of branch and Constituency delegates than conference. Council has the authority to do anything Conference can do — subject to its being overruled by Conference. This means it can — and does — make party policy out of view of the press and television. Since it is also smaller and meets more frequently than Conference, its debates have more coherence. Assembly has two delegates from each Constituency. It lacks the authority of Council. In a way, it is a 'talk shop'. The party rules charge it with the duty of 'evolve and review policies'. But its decisions about policy are not official party policy unless they are passed by either Council or Conference.

It seems to me that the SNP procedure has both public relations and policy advantages. On the one hand it allows a democratically elected body to have detailed and serious discussions about policies — usually one or two areas of policy are concentrated on in a year — while on the other hand it enables contentious issues to be discussed out of sight of the public. Because the party has such a complicated route of policy-making, the debates which it holds in public each year at Conference have more the air of a public affirmation than a debate.

The real problem which the SNP is encountering is that it has been making policy for an independent Scotland which does not exist. This gives its policy statements an unreal air. Everything can be promised, each interest accommodated with little trouble because all know in their hearts that what they are debating makes little difference. At the 1978 Annual Conference, for instance, the Party adopted a document: *Post-Independence Economic Strategy* which was all too obviously a compound of several different committees' drafts on the same subject. Paragraph 4, for instance, began:

'Economic strategy is a combination of measures, some of which will have an immediate effect, while others will have an increasing effect in the longer term. On the achievement of independence, measures will be attaining the following objectives.'

Paragraph 5, however, began:

'On the achievement of independence, measures will be immediately adopted which will have an increasing effect in the longer term in attaining the following objectives.'

The document continues in that fashion with whole series of successive paragraphs containing roughly — but not exactly — similar thoughts on single topics. If policy-making is to have any meaning, it must result from a deliberate decision to reject some options. It is not clear that the SNP is fulfilling this criteria. But at least by the time it comes to discuss such documents in public, it has agreed within itself on just what it is going to say. Policies on subjects which might give rise to unflattering comment in the press can sometimes be decided at National Council and never brought to Conference: Defence policy is one.

It is not unreasonable to expect that the coming of the Assembly will make this kind of polite settlement of contentious issues in private less possible. Policies will matter more and hence people will be less polite about losing.

9. *Coalition Formation:*

Some features of the Scotland Act conspire with aspects of contemporary Scottish party competition to force the Assembly's Executive to consider forming coalitions from time to time. One of the most important of these features is the system of four-yearly elections. The need to hold an election every four years, whether or not the Assembly agrees to an interim election, will remove from the Executive the possibility that it will be able to call elections at times when its party is popular with the electorate and avoid calling them when it is unpopular. Without this possibility, the leaders of the largest party — even when that party has a small overall majority of Assembly seats — will have to think seriously about forming a coalition with some other party in order to remain in office.

The committee system will affect this thinking too. For with a developed committee system, back-bench Assembly members will not be so completely tied to their party Whips for advancement. Without this tie, they may be more independent than MPs are and less willing to vote for the Executive of their party. Thus weakened, the Executive may have an additional incentive to form a coalition.

At the same time, the Scottish electorate has been dividing its favours between the major parties in roughly equal thirds for the past few years. If this pattern continues, it is unlikely that any party will get an overwhelming majority of seats and it is certainly possible that no party will have a majority at all. In that latter case, there will have to be some kind of arrangement between the parties about the formation and support in the Assembly, of the Executive.

In some cultures the method of choosing the First Secretary of the Assembly would also make coalitions likely. The First Secretary is to be chosen by the Assembly. If no one party has a majority of seats, it will be tempting for the leaders of the second and third parties to form a coalition between themselves and some members of the largest party. If, say, Labour had 73 of the 150 Assembly seats, it might be tempting to the Conservative and SNP leaders to form a coalition with a small group — say 10 Labour Assembly members — and make one of the ten First Secretary. This would divide the Labour Party badly and the First Secretary would be the creature of the coalition partners. Some such coalitions have emerged from time to time in European countries. But British politicians and the British electorate have no

experience of this kind of compromise and might not like it. It's too
clever. That is the problem of coalition formation writ large.

We have before us the unhappy examples of Glasgow District
Council since 1977 and several other smaller Councils in which no
party had an overall majority. No party was willing to form a formal
coalition or even a pact with the others. This leads to weak, vacillatory,
and indecisive government. But the party leaders cannot be blamed too
much for their unwillingness to get together. Their electorate would
almost certainly not stand for deals, particularly private deals, with
other parties.

The support which the various parties enjoy from their electors is
simply too weak for the leaders to comfortably enter into coalitions
with other parties. The loss of popularity suffered by the Liberal Party
after its leadership made a pact with the Labour Government in 1977
is clear enough warning of the fate of small partners in coalitions. We
suffer here from the disadvantages of the mobility and tolerance of
Scotland. Were Scotland divided rigidly between classes, or nations, or
sects, and if each group had its own party, there would be little
possibility of supporters of one party deserting to another because of a
deal done by the party leaders. There are some societies which are
divided socially in this manner and which, nevertheless, support very
complicated patterns of coalition formation over long periods of time:
the Netherlands is often cited as one such society. But Scotland — as
the recent shifts in voting patterns show — lacks such solid identifica-
tion. Any party leader — to recur to my previous example — the ten
Labour Assembly members who formed a pact with the Tory and
Nationalist devils — would risk losing all support at the next election.
So would the Conservative and SNP leaders who dealt with him.

Coalition formation between a large party and either the Liberal
Party and any Independent Assembly members would however, be a
most attractive alternative. The Liberals would not be unacceptable
partners to any of the large parties. Independents would be suspect to a
Labour group but couldn't categorically rule a coalition there out.
However, Independent members who represent rural seats might be
highly acceptable to Conservative or Scottish National Party Assembly
groups. The problem is that the Liberal Party has been badly squeezed
by the electorate in the period after its pact with the Labour Government and might not survive in sufficiently large number to make
coalitions possible. Independents are being squeezed out of even local
government and would be most unlikely to win Assembly seats — at
least for the first few Assembly elections. Nevertheless, if there is an

Assembly group of six to ten Liberal members and a few Independents where no party has a clear majority of seats the small parties might have a real role.

But the outlook for the Liberals and the Independents is not bright, and if we are to have coalitions, they will most likely be coalitions between two of the three large parties. The leaders of these parties owe it to themselves and their parties, not to mention to anyone else, to begin to make their parties think about the need for coalitions. Otherwise we risk suffering a series of weak, divided and vacillatory Assembly Executives. Such weakness will not lead to good government for Scotland. It will not improve the reputation of devolution with either the Scottish or English people.

Chapter 7

Westminster and the Assembly

GEOFFREY SMITH

THERE are three possible reasons why people of very different views may want to see a Scottish Assembly established. One is the hope that it may prove to be a stepping-stone to full independence: that is naturally the attitude of most Nationalists. The second is the belief that it will be a more acceptable and efficient form of government because it will bring the process of decision-making nearer to the people directly affected. The third is the assumption that most people in Scotland want a form of constitutional change that will give greater recognition to Scotland's distinctive identity, and that Scotland will be a happier partner within the United Kingdom if there is a positive response to this wish.

For those who take the first of these positions it may not be necessary to have smooth relations between the Assembly and Westminster. Some of them will wish to have good relations simply because they think this will lead to the greater welfare of the Scottish people and because they would prefer full independence to evolve in a co-operative spirit between the two countries. But there are others who will, quite logically, if to my mind regrettably, not wish the Assembly to give general satisfaction for fear that it may then prove to be a lasting solution. From that point of view, a fair amount of tension between the Assembly and Westminster would be positively helpful.

Those who favour devolution for the second reason would certainly prefer to have good relations between the Assembly and Westminster, but they would want to have devolution anyway because they believe it to offer a superior form of government. For them co-operation between Edinburgh and London must be eminently desirable, but it is not logically essential. A degree of tension might even be regarded as stimulating for both sides.

But for those of us who look favourably upon devolution for the ensuring that the leading politicians on both sides did keep in reasonably frequent contact. It might be useful in bringing them together when there was not anything very dramatic for them to talk about, which is another way of saying before problems have reached an explosive stage. But the fewer the parties there are to consultation the less the formal procedures matter.

It is for that reason that comparisons with the German Lander or with the federal-provincial conferences in Canada are not so relevant as they might seem. In both those cases a federal Government is seeking to maintain regular contact with a number of subordinate administrations. Therefore the procedures for consultation have to some extent to be formalised. They all have to be brought together at the same time and the same place. It will be different with a Scottish Assembly. There may be a Welsh Assembly as well, and even conceivably at some time in the future another Northern Irish Assembly. But in any case all these Assemblies would have different powers, and consultation with them would not be on the same footing.

So it is unlikely that the Joint Council for Scotland will play a particularly important role. If there are urgent conflicts, British and Scottish ministers would meet anyway; and such a council could not meet sufficiently often to provide the necessary day-to-day consultation. Much of that will take place between officials. It will be argued that this will be all the easier with the Civil Servants advising the Assembly still being part of the UK Civil Service. But that is unlikely to be of much practical consequence for this purpose.

Even though they will be members of the same Civil Service, it would not be feasible for them to be members of that web of inter-departmental committees which is such a central part of the decision-making process in Whitehall. If they were, it would immediately be said that devolution was a sham and that behind the political facade the administrative control of London was undiminished. But the Assembly Civil Servants will still want to be closely in touch with that process, they will want to feed into it the views and special considerations of the Scottish administration. How can that be done?

One possible answer is that the telephone and the shuttle air service will be enough. The means will be available for Civil Servants on both sides to keep in as close contact as they wish. But plausible though that may seem, it will not be sufficient. In relations between the two countries, the Scottish vice is an inferiority complex; the English vice is insensitivity. Logic suggests that English Civil Servants will be so aware that in certain fields the decisions taken in one country will have a strong, though often a complex, impact on the other that they will keep Scottish considerations very much in mind. But experience indicates that they are all too likely to regard what happens in Scotland as a boring irrelevance unless they are subjected to the pleasure of frequent reminders. What form should these reminders take?

In theory there could be a system of joint committees paralleling the inter-departmental committees in Whitehall. But that would be too cumbersome, and certainly too time-consuming for English Civil Servants. If such committees were ever set up, they would be a poor medium of consultation because senior English Civil Servants would attend them so infrequently. It would be better and more probable for the linking role to be undertaken by the rump of the present Scottish Office, the Civil Servants still serving the Secretary of State for Scotland.

Many supporters of devolution have maintained that the Office ought to be abolished altogether. But that is tantamount to arguing that a different form of devolution should have been adopted, which may be correct but is beside the point at this stage. Given the number of government functions in Scotland that are not to be devolved, it is inevitable that a Scottish Office should be retained. These responsibilities could not, or at any rate would not, all be carried out satisfactorily by UK departments. There will, moreover, be positive advantages in having Scottish Civil Servants still operating within the Whitehall nexus.

This will be an Office deliberately in search of a role. It will retain some important administrative tasks, especially in the economic sphere, but it is bound to be acutely conscious of what it has lost. Most senior officials in the present Scottish Office, including the most senior, can be expected to move over to the Assembly. The psychology of the Office that is left may well be that of a department that is on the way down. That is certainly how it is liable to be regarded in Whitehall unless it devises a new role for itself. It might set itself up to monitor the activities of the Assembly, so that it could offer detailed advice to the Secretary of State on when and where to intervene. But if it does too much in that direction the outcome will be disastrous.

It will play a much more valuable part if it seeks to be the mediator between the Scottish Executive and Whitehall. The Scottish Office can expect in the future, as it can now, to be represented on all Whitehall committees, and its members will be heard with more attention if they serve as constant reminders of opinion within the Scottish administration. There would be no constitutional conflict in such a role, any more than there was in the days of the old Commonwealth Relations

Office or than there is now when the Foreign Office reminds other departments of the relevance of overseas opinion to the decisions that will be taken in London.

This would obviously not be an exclusive line of communication between the Assembly and Whitehall. On a good many issues it would be natural for there to be direct contact between Assembly Civil Servants and the appropriate Whitehall department. On matters of major conflict, senior ministers would no doubt be brought in. But on a day-by-day basis the Scottish Office could perform an essential function by ensuring that inter-departmental committees were kept in touch with all Scottish considerations — not just those affecting non-devolved subjects — and by providing the necessary feedback. The success of devolution could be much affected by this unseen part of the system.

Another part of the system that needs to be seen as little as possible is the financing of the Assembly. To put it like this is admittedly a plea for perfection. This may well prove to be the most difficult area in practice. If the financing arrangements do not work well it will undermine the whole devolution scheme and poison relations between the Assembly and Westminster. It is given to few governments in the Western world to please their electorates for any length of time these days, and there is no reason to believe that the Scottish Executive will be an exception to this rule. But will it be able to export its unpopularity to put the blame for its failings on the parsimony of London? That will almost certainly happen if the financing of the Assembly remains a matter of continuing controversy, which is what one would expect unless the greatest care is taken. The natural reaction of a beleaguered Scottish Executive will be to say: 'Poor housing? Inferior roads? Ill-equipped schools? Ah, if only London would give us the money. Look what they have down south'.

The denial of tax-raising powers to the Assembly will mean that everything will depend on the Block Grant. Its size will determine the scope of activity for a Scottish administration. That will make it hard for members of the Scottish Executive ever to accept that they have been given enough. But a still worse danger is that the method of negotiating the Grant could restrict the Assembly's freedom of action. This would happen if a Scottish administration had to justify the sum it sought by pointing to the merits of the programmes on which it would be spent. The bargaining on money would then all too easily slide into a negotiation over policies, and Assembly ministers would find that they could extract more from the Treasury if it was proposed to spend the money in certain directions rather than others. A roads programme to keep pace with what was being done in England might, for example, be more difficult to refuse than a new experiment in health care. In theory it would always be available to a Scottish administration, once it had got the money, to spend it in a different way — but that would hardly strengthen its hand for the next round of negotiations. It would in fact be beholden to the Treasury in much the same way as the big spending departments of Whitehall.

If this is the way in which the system develops, it will be contrary to the whole spirit and purpose of devolution. It will be bad enough if there is even annual haggling over the size of the Grant. The natural tactic for the Scottish Executive would be to put pressure on the Treasury by mobilising Scottish opinion, which would mean in practice a succession of calculated leaks to the Scottish press on the minimum required to give Scotland a fair deal. It would be sensible negotiation always to overstate that minimum, so year by year Scottish newspapers, television and radio would be filled with stories of how once again Scotland had failed to gain its just desserts. Or alternatively there would be crows of delight at the negotiating triumph of the Scottish Executive, which would hardly placate the outraged regions of England suspecting that Scotland had once more stolen a march on them.

It is to avoid these dangers that the Government now intends to propose to the Scottish Executive that a four-yearly needs-based formula should be negotiated to determine the relative shares of public expenditure in the devolved fields for Scotland and the rest of the UK. This will be no simple task. The difficulty of devising any formula that will be economically just is set out in the next chapter on 'Financial Control and Responsibility'. The economic tools may well not be available to measure the relative needs of different areas with objective precision. The selection of the ingredients for any formula is liable to be too subjective to pass the searching scrutiny of the economist.

But from a political standpoint one may have a more modest goal. We do not need a formula that is made in heaven: it will be enough to have one that will work on earth. It is a great advantage that, as is shown in the next chapter, the relative shares of public expenditure in the devolved fields between Scotland and the rest of the UK have been reasonably stable over the years. So what one needs is a formula that will clothe this political reality in objective economic garments. There is no reason why the coming of devolution should lead to an increase or a decline in the proportion of public expenditure coming to Scotland, and the purpose of a formula should be to secure the continuation of that economic balance with the minimum of political hassle. Never mind if the formula has economic imperfections so long as it achieves that end, which means that it should be based so far as possible on criteria that do not have to be changed even if the actual figures vary from year to year — size of population, age distribution, geographical area, incidence of disease and so forth.

Even such a formula would not solve all problems. What the Government has in mind is one for total public expenditure in the devolved fields, which would therefore include spending financed by local authority rates and borrowing. The formula would consequently not directly determine the size of the Grant to the Assembly — though it could be made to do so by allowing for these other sources of finance to provide for a regular fixed proportion of the total. Table 1 in chapter 8 shows that in 1975-76 local authority rates and borrowing were together equal to 30% of total expenditure in Scotland in the devolved fields. If this was considered an appropriate proportion, it would mean that for every £100 that was Scotland's share of public expenditure in the devolved fields, £70 would go to the Assembly in the Block Grant. The assumption would be that local authority rates and borrowing would make up the other £30.

If rates in Scotland dropped below this national figure then spending in the devolved fields would be lower too, but that would be the result of deliberate decisions by democratically elected public bodies in Scotland. It would be equally justifiable on the same principle if local authorities decided to levy rates at a higher level in order to provide more generous services.

The formula would still not prescribe the absolute level of the Grant in any year. That would depend on the total sum made available by the UK for spending in these fields. This would mean that certain policy adjustments for England would have unforeseen consequences for Scotland. If there was a switch of expenditure away from schools in England (which are a devolved responsibility in Scotland) towards universities (which are not devolved), that would lead to a lower Block Grant for the Assembly. There is no way round this particular problem: it simply points the need for the Scottish Executive to be able to insert its views into the policy-making process in London through the closest possible consultation.

If the estimates are to be expressed in due course largely in the form of cash limits, that should reduce the number of supplementary estimates, which would mean that the formula would not have to be invoked for chopping and changing the Block Grant two or three times a year. But changes in spending needs may occur in the course of a year because of deliberate changes in government policy. Could any formula provide for an economic emergency?

What if a Chancellor were to decide that no new contracts were to be signed by government departments for three months as an economy measure? Should he apply that restriction to devolved activities in Scotland and be accused of interfering in the Assembly's legitimate procedures? Should he exclude the Assembly from the restriction and be accused of not insisting upon equality of sacrifice? Or should he simply adjust the Block Grant and hope that the eventual economic effects might not be too different in Scotland and England, even though a Scottish administration might decide to cut current rather than capital expenditure? The third of these options would be the best, but one has to allow for the fact that either a misguided judgment of economic necessity or political pressure from English opinion might lead a Chancellor to act differently. In which case he will be taking risks with the stability of the devolution scheme unless he shows considerble gifts of political presentation.

Relations between the Assembly and Westminster are bound, however, to be affected as much by political appearances as by the smoothness with which the process of government actually proceeds. The most important aspect in this connection has come to be known as the West Lothian question in recognition of the persistence of the MP for that constituency, Mr Tam Dalyell. This concerns the position of Scottish MPs after devolution. There is really a double problem: one will be the resentment of English MPs if policy for England on subjects that have been devolved for Scotland is determined by the balance of representation from Scotland. This would mean that policy for England in these fields was being settled by Scottish MPs, whereas English MPs were able to have no influence over policy in these same fields in Scotland. The second problem is that Scottish MPs may not like having to leave a whole range of social policies to the Assembly, especially as some of these matters are the principal concern of many voters. Will Scottish MPs come to feel that they have been pushed to one side?

Both of these problems were presented in precisely the same form in the case of Northern Ireland for so long as there was an Assembly at Stormont, but with one significant exception. The number of Ulster MPs at Westminster, being confined to 12, was so small that they were not expected to hold the balance of power. Nor did they ever — quite. Neither the Attlee Government of 1950-51 nor the Wilson government, had they gained the support of the Unionists, might have had to go to the country again quite so quickly. But neither of those occasions occurred until the anomaly had existed long enough to be sanctified by time.

The best hope must be that there will be a similar breathing space after devolution comes into operation. But as there are 71 Scottish MPs, there is clearly a much greater chance of their tipping the balance at Westminster — as indeed they do at the moment. One way to avoid this would be to apply the in-and-out principle that was initially in Gladstone's second Irish Home Rule Bill. This provided for all Parliamentary business to be divided into Imperial, British and Irish matters, with Irish members having the right to take part only on Imperial and Irish questions. That principle did not survive sustained examination then and there is no reason to believe that it could be applied satisfactorily now.

Indeed, Parliament has inserted a muddled modification of this principle into the Act. This provides that where a Bill dealing with a subject that in Scotland has been devolved to the Assembly receives a Second Reading in the House of Commons only because of the votes of Scottish MPs, then the House must vote again a fortnight later if the Second Reading is to be confirmed. This would be a cumbersome procedure which would be unlikely to affect the outcome except when the House is very closely divided, but which would keep on drawing attention to the anomalous position of the Scottish members. It is a trouble-making provision that would be better ignored.

There is a chance that it might be. The Act also specifies that this clause shall not come into operation unless it has been approved by a resolution of the House of Commons. If there is a Conservative majority in the House there would be no need to activate this clause because the Scottish MPs would not hold the balance, and if they do hold the balance there will almost certainly be a Labour majority in the House who would have no incentive to weaken their strength by bringing such a rule into effect. It will be best if it is left quietly in abeyance while Parliament comes to terms with the existence of the Assembly. That would be somewhat easier to achieve if the number of Scottish MPs was reduced. Once there is an Assembly there can be no justification for the continued over-representation of Scotland at Westminster. If Scotland were to be represented on the same basis as England, that would still leave Scotland with 57 members, according to the calculations of the Kilbrandon Commission. But the symbolic effect of the change might do something to reconcile English opinion to the anomaly.

The risk that Scottish MPs will themselves feel at a loss should not be dismissed as a matter of consequence only to them. If it happens, it would weaken the voice of Scotland at Westminster, not least because it would be a disincentive to people of calibre in Scotland standing for Parliament. This would mean that Scottish opinion would find itself represented increasingly by the Assembly throughout the whole range of public affairs, which would not necessarily be a bad thing but would be different from the political balance envisaged in devolution. It would be a further step in the direction of federalism.

But the extent to which the position of Scottish MPs will be changed can be exaggerated. Because there is already so much administrative devolution, and so much separate legislation for Scotland, they have for years been effectively debarred from a number of UK offices. No Scottish MP now could be Secretary of State for Education or responsible for English housing. In one respect Scottish MPs might even be in a more favourable position at Westminster after devolution. Much of their time is now taken up with exclusively Scottish business which most English MPs find excrutiatingly boring. After devolution there will be less purely Scottish legislation going through Parliament and more need and opportunity for Scottish MPs to take a broader interest in British affairs, which might possibly bring them more into the mainstream of Parliamentary life if they seize the chance. It will be worth considering after a while, for example, whether it is still necessary to have the Scottish Grand Committee and the Scottish Standing Committee.

There are other procedural questions which will need to be examined. After the establishment of Stormont, the speaker of the House of Commons ruled that devolved subjects could not be raised at Westminster but should be addressed to the appropriate minister in Northern Ireland. There is much to be said for a similar rule in the case of Scotland now, if it is feasible. There would be the difficulty — much greater with Scotland than with Northern Ireland — of determining, often presumably on the spur of the moment, whether a question referred to a subject that had or had not been devolved. MPs would also want to have the right to question UK ministers not only on their use of the power of override but on their failure to use that power. But it might be possible to draw a distinction between questioning a minister on the exercise of his responsibility and discussing the substance of Assembly policy.

Such a distinction could be made effective only if MPs exercised a reasonable sense of restraint. But that will be necessary to make devolution work at all. If the House of Commons wishes, it can insist upon the expenditure of the Block Grant by the Assembly being open to inspection by the Public Accounts Committee in London, which would provoke a political storm. But an amendment to that effect was not pressed as the Bill was going through Parliament, and unless the House is in search of a conflict it will continue to leave well alone. The success of devolution will depend in no small measure upon British ministers, back-bench MPs and Civil Servants refraining from exercising to the full the powers that will still nominally be theirs. Just as devolution could be wrecked by a Scottish administration that did not wish it to work and deliberately sought conflict with London, so it could also be destroyed if Westminster and Whitehall do not abide by the spirit of the settlement — which means allowing Edinburgh to get on with its tasks without interference unless absolutely necessary.

In theory it could be argued that the Assembly should show similar restraint by refraining from airing its views on matters that are the responsibility of the UK Parliament. One cannot imagine many debates of this nature that would take the form of an extended congratulation: as a rule they would be occasions for beefing. But it would be unrealistic to expect the Assembly to keep a vow of silence on such central questions of political concern as the general management of the Scottish economy.

In this as in other respects it is no use expecting relations between the Assembly and Westminster to be conducted in an atmosphere of monastic virtue. Conflict is the stuff of politics when politicians are engaged in the exercise of real power, as they will be in this case. What matters is that conflict should not be taken to the point of rupture. If it is the will of the Scottish people to rupture the relationship, then no political devices in the world will be able to maintain it indefinitely. But if that is not their will, then the task over devolution is to establish arrangements that will prevent either side stumbling inadvertently down a path they do not wish to take.

Chapter 8

Financial Control and Responsibility

P. M. JACKSON

Introduction

THE majority of countries in the world are to some degree federal in their structure of government. Of these the UK remains one of the few unitary states, being centrally governed from Westminster. The devolution Bill which will give limited legislative and administrative authority to a newly created Scottish Assembly will not result in the creation of a federation within the UK. Many of the problems which will arise when the provisions contained in the Bill are put into practice, are due to the fact that devolution in the UK will be seen to be partial. The UK will be a 'semi-federal system in a semi-unitary state'. Not least of the problems will be those of an economic or a financial nature.

Political and administrative discussions of devolution cannot be divorced from the financial arrangements which will enable the Scottish Assembly to achieve its objectives. Nor would it be at all sensible, especially in the age of the 'new political economy', to discuss the financing of the new Assembly without paying proper regard to the political and administrative structures which are proposed. The economic, financial and political dimensions of constitutional change are intertwined and this was recognised in the *Memorandum of Dissent to the Kilbrandon Commission* (Cmnd. 5460, 1973) when it was pointed out that ' the principle of a substantial equality of political rights and obligations throughout the United Kingdom carries with it, in our view, important economic and financial rights . . . This is because the ultimate purpose of political rights is to enable people to provide for themselves a fuller, freer and richer life than might otherwise be possible'. (paragraph 127).

In this chapter we shall set out the proposed financial arrangements for the Scottish Assembly, paying particular attention to the problems and the confusions which were apparent amongst some members of both the House of Commons and the House of Lords during the discussions of these financial arrangements in the Bill.

There is no suggestion in the Bill that the financial arrangements for the Assembly are fixed for ever, nor is there any reason to suppose that the Assembly will adopt and maintain the current Westminster model of public sector financial management and control. The political, administrative and financial systems of the Assembly will develop over time, with the first few years of development being the most crucial for the subsequent drive to maturity. It is, therefore, essential right from the beginning to recognise the limitations of the present proposals and to ensure that there exists some mechanism by which development or the lack of it in one sphere of the Assembly's business, does not constrain developments elsewhere. Given the importance of the financial constraint, we must be absolutely clear about the limitations which the financial arrangements will place on the realisation of the objectives of devolution. If the financing of the Scottish Assembly does prove to be a problem what arrangements will be made to change them? These questions will be addressed in this paper and it will be shown that the financing of the assembly will be one of the most contentious areas between the Scottish Assembly and Westminster.

The Assembly does, however, offer a potentially exciting development in public sector financial management and control. Given the more general criticisms about the role and the management of the UK public sector, the Assembly offers a unique upportunity to set down a more efficient internal system for the allocation of resources along with new systems of Scottish public expenditure monitoring and control. Indeed, as will be shown below, one of the consequences of the proposed financial arrangements will be the need for the Scottish Assembly to have a tighter control on its finances; a view which is not shared by many who discussed the Bill during the committee stage!

The Political Economy of Devolution

In order that our assessment of the financial provisions of the Bill may be structured we present the following framework. Any change in an existing system, be it political or financial, must be judged against the objectives which the system seeks to achieve. Moreover, that change can be discussed in terms of the net cost (benefit minus cost) of achieving the stated objective. It is, therefore, incumbent upon us to consider the objectives of the devolved Assembly and then to ask: 'Will the financial provisions of the Bill enable these objectives to be achieved and at what cost?' To see the force of this question we imagine that one paradoxical answer to it could be that the present financial arrangements which exist under our highly centralised and unitary system would serve the interests of the Scots better than those which are proposed! Clearly in that case the financial provisions of the Bill will constrain the achievement of its primary objectives, and indeed confound it by unwittingly or otherwise resulting in very little actual change. Devolution could then become an hallucination in which the structure of government is changed by shuffling the cards in the pack but leaving the power relations of the face cards intact.

Stated broadly, the objectives of devolution are to transmit to an elected Scottish Assembly the legislative and administrative authority to allocate resources in such a way that they will conform to the majority of preferences of a Scottish electorate. Such an arrangement will allow policies to be formulated and carried out in Scotland which are more appropriate to the needs of Scotland.

As such, the demand for devolution is a political issue. It is about the best way of organising governments and as such, it is an expression of preference from a section of the electorate within a region for independence in decision-making. Such a demand for independence arises from a number of sources amongst which will be included the belief that the particular disadvantages of the region (social and economic) are directly related to decisions or the lack of decisions from the 'centre', and an inherent value placed on own self-government etc. Whether or not the advantages believed to flow from independence are real or imaginary is an open question which can only be answered by appealing to the facts. Thus any *a priori* analysis can only set out the pros and cons, all of which are equally forceful in the debate until such time as numbers and magnitudes are revealed and placed against them.

Other advantages following from devolution, apart from the above, could be that if the centre of decision-making is closer to those affected by policy decisions then there exists a greater chance for control over the policy-making process, including the role played by bureaucracy. Thus the establishment of a Scottish Assembly *may* allow the Scottish bureaucracy to be put under greater scrutiny than has been so in the past.

There are many factors which influence the welfare of the electorate, not least of these being the provisions made in a government's budget. One legitimate question which can therefore be asked is: 'How will the budget of a Scottish Assembly serve the interests of the Scottish electorate and what will that budget do which the budget of the present

Westminster Government cannot?' The budget is the vehicle by which the policies of the Assembly will be transmitted. A budget is more than just a financial statement. In many respects the budget can be read as a statement revealing the nation's preferences for education, for the elimination of poverty, for the improvement of the physical environment, and for the preservation of its cultural and artistic heritage. The acquisition of these goods and services requires resources and funds which are stated in the budget.

At a greater level of detail, however, any budgetary system aims to serve a number of objectives. These are:

(a) *Allocative Efficiency:* this objective is not confined to the narrow concept of ensuring that public expenditure is allocated at minimum cost. Rather it is concerned with using the budget as a *means* to achieve an efficient allocation of resources throughout the economy. This includes improving the growth rate of the economy, the stimulation of investment, industrial reconstruction and regeneration, retraining of labour, promoting regional economic balance and controlling environmental degradation. The budget is also used to ensure an efficient 'mix' of resources between the public and private sectors of the economy.

(b) *Distributional Efficiency:* within any society the prevailing distribution of resources (human and physical capital) and purchasing power (income) may not be considered to be 'just' or 'fair' (however defined). The budget can be used to bring the actual distribution closer to the desired. This is done by using tax and public expenditure policies.

(c) *Stabilisation of the Economy:* the economic functions of promoting industrial growth etc., which were outlined under the heading of *Allocative Efficiency*, relate to the longer term or the supply/structural aspects of the economy. In the short term, however, an economy is faced with problems of unemployment, inflation, balance of payments difficulties etc . . . The budget is used in an attempt to bring these forces into a stable balance. This is done by changes in public spending and taxation (i.e., fiscal policy) or via changes in interest rates and the money supply (i.e., monetary policy and not strictly budgetary policy).

The point of setting out these budgetary functions at length is that we need to be quite clear about the budgetary powers that have been devolved to the Scottish Assembly. For example, which particular objectives can the Assembly seek to achieve, given the budgetary and financial resources that have been devolved to it? Given that the

Under the present system, public expenditure in Scotland is made up of Scottish local government expenditure (capital and current), Scottish Office centrally administered expenditures and Scottish public corporations expenditures. These are financed in the case of local authorities from local rates, local user charges (e.g., rents), local borrowing and from the Rate Support Grant which is paid to local authorities from central government taxation via the Scottish Office. Scottish Office expenditure and subsidies paid to the Scottish public corporations are financed from central government tax revenues and borrowings.

Following the establishment of the Scottish Assembly, Scottish public expenditures will arise from the services devolved to the Assembly and from non-devolved services which will continue to be administered through the office of the Secretary of State for Scotland. Assuming that the present structure of local government will continue after devolution:

(a) *Local Government Devolved Services* (e.g., housing, education, social services) will be financed from local rates and the financial transfers between the Scottish Assembly and the Scottish local governments, which may be of the kind currently embodied in the present Rate Support Grant and specific grants. Capital expenditures and current account deficits will be financed from borrowing drawn from the same source as at present.

(b) *Local Government Non-devolved Services* (essentially police) will be financed from local rates, charges, Rate Support Grant and specific grants paid by the Scottish Office (i.e., from the Secretary of State's Votes) and from borrowing, for which approval will be sought from the Scottish Office.

(c) *Central Government Devolved Services* will be financed from the Block Grant, from charges and from borrowing from the Scottish Loans Fund.

Since it is only the financing of devolved service expenditures that are of interest to us, we should be clear about the sources of funds to finance such expenditures. The revenue to finance devolved expenditure is made up from the Block Grant, local authority rates, borrowing, and user charges (i.e., prices paid for public services such as rents or prescription charges). It is of interest to note that the Assembly, by withholding grants to Scottish local authorities, could increase the availability of funds for centrally administered services. This would increase the potential flexibility of the Assembly's budget constraint but would put pressure on Scottish local authorities and clearly affect

Assembly/local government relationships, a point which is considered in greater detail below.

The amount of flexibility and hence freedom which the Scottish Assembly has over the size of total devolved expenditures is dependent upon the degrees of freedom it has over the determination of its budget constraint, and this in turn depends upon the discretion which it has at its disposal to vary the components of the source of funds.

We now turn to the examination of these components.

The Block Fund

The most important source of revenue for the Scottish Consolidated Fund will be that arising from the Block Fund allocation. Table 1 shows that, on the assumptions used for the exercise in Cmnd. 6890, the Block Fund contributed 66.3% of total Scottish Assembly revenue. It is, therefore, important to discuss how this Grant allocation will be determined and what problems these decisions may pose.

From the outset there are two sets of questions which may be asked. First, how is the Grant most likely to be determined and second, how *should* it be determined? We shall, in the meantime, delay answering the second question.

The size of the Block Grant will be determined by Parliament each year along with all other items of public expenditure such as the Department of Education and Science's budget and that for Defence and so on. The Block Fund Order will be placed before Parliament for debate and on the outcome of the voting of that debate will depend the size of the Scottish Assembly's Block Fund allocation. That allocation (i.e., the Grant) will be determined (i.e., approved by Parliament) for the next year only. At the same time a Borrowing Limit Order will also be placed before Parliament for discussion and approval. Having been determined, the Block Grant is then paid into the Scottish Consolidated Fund in instalments.

Whilst the above paragraph outlines the formal procedure for voting a Block Fund allocation, it begs most of the interesting questions not least of which is how are the expenditure data contained in the Block Fund Order and the Borrowing Limit Order arrived at? It should be made perfectly clear at this stage that at no time has there been any precise statement made by the Government on the *exact* details of the Grant determination process. This is right and proper since it does not automatically close off options which the new Scottish Assembly will be able to consider. Moreover, it leaves the maximum feasible degree of openness for new arrangements to emerge between the Assembly and Westminster. We can, however, gain some insight to government thinking by looking at the statements which have been made in Cmnd. 6890 (especially paragraphs 66-78) and from the discussion of the Bill as it passed through the committee stage.

The basis upon which the size of the Block Grant will be decided will depend upon an assessment of relative Scottish needs. By stating the problem in this way it is hoped that the process of Grant determination will conform to the desirable characteristics of any Grant system; namely that it (a) should be objective, (b) should match up to agreed standards of equity, and (c) should be sufficiently flexible over time by paying regard to changing circumstances. Having said that, however, we are left with the empirical problem of assessing needs and with the question of how alternative pragmatic approaches to dealing with the technical problems of need-assessment may frustrate the realisation of the objectives of the Scottish Assembly. It is worthwhile dwelling for a moment on this issue of how we judge the efficiency of the Grant system because it is not without relevance for the whole debate. The features of an efficient Grant system are not neutral. They depend upon whose interests are being serviced. Thus what constitutes a 'good' Grant system from the Scottish Assembly's perspective may not conform to that of Westminster. It depends upon the objective that the Grant must serve and, if it has to satisfy many objectives, which are incompatible with one another, then the likely result is political conflict.

Basing the Block Grant upon an assessment of relative needs recognises that different regions of the UK, by virtue of their special local circumstances, give rise to higher unit costs of service provision. This is the basis upon which the current local authority Rate Support Grant is determined. Taking into account differences in the size and composition of the population, its sparsity, the relative amount of unemployment, poverty and the housing conditions of the region as well as its general topology, the size of the Grant is thereby considered on the objective assessment of these conditions within a region.

Given our current knowledge about the factors which give rise to public expenditures it is not technically possible to form a precise relationship between needs-variations between regions and public expenditure variations. Moreover, there is much debate about whether or not the objective indices which are currently available do indeed reflect our subjective notions of what constitutes needs. It should, therefore, be clear that there is no technically simple or mechanistic procedure for determining public expenditure in Scotland compared to that in England on the basis of relative expenditure/need measurement. Whilst regression analysis and unit cost accounting provide management data, which may be used in Grant decision-making, these data limitations must be recognised and treated with caution (see the *Layfield Committee Report,* Cmnd. 6453, Appendix 7).

The size of the Grant not only depends upon expenditure demands but also upon a region's ability to pay (taxable capacity) to meet these needs. Thus the Grant is also in part based upon the principle of regional equalisation which can be summarised as follows: 'Areas with large needs, involuntarily high unit costs of service provision and a relatively low tax base should not be penalised but have these characteristics compensated for by, in effect, fiscal transfers from other areas.' Thus, each area 'should have the opportunity if it so chooses to provide services to a common standard and . . . should be able to finance that level of provision by imposing a common burden of taxation'.

In deciding upon a figure to put into the Block Fund Order for Parliament's decision, an important element in the calculation will be an assessment of Scottish expenditure needs relative to the rest of the UK and relative to Scotland's ability to pay. But who is to do the assessment and how? Two possible answers to this question will be set out and then assessed.

'Centralist' vs. 'Co-operative' Approaches to Block Fund
Determination

The two models which we shall consider are extremes and as such, have been chosen to emphasise the principles as well as the problems involved. In the first model we imagine that Westminster, and the Treasury in particular, will take each item of Scottish Executive devolved expenditure and scrutinize it closely. The Scottish Assembly at the appropriate point of the budget cycle each year would make a detailed request for a budget covering the next year on the basis of its own forecasts and assessments of spending needs. The Treasury would then scrutinize the elements of the budget request, comparing it against its assessment of Scottish needs and calling upon the Scottish Assembly, where necessary, to justify its requests. For example, the Treasury may request the Scottish Assembly to account for variations in the standard and provision of devolved services as compared to equivalent English services.

There are a number of issues which are thrown up by this model and it is best to identify them by means of a series of questions, mainly

Let us first be clear that we understand the rule. It could be that Scotland will receive 15% of English equivalent public expenditure to finance its devolved services. The important point is to note that the Block Fund would be based on 'equivalent expenditure' i.e., on the expenditure on services which are comparable to those which have been devolved to the Scottish Assembly. If, instead, it had been based on total UK public expenditure then the Grant would have increased along with increases on expenditure on non-devolved services such as defence, pensions, unemployment benefits and so on; this would have violated all reasonable principles of equity and justice.

Table 2 shows the ratio of Scottish Assembly expenditure on devolved services to English equivalent expenditures.

It is readily seen in Table 2 that the ratio of Scottish Assembly devolved expenditures to English equivalent expenditure has been (in real terms) fairly stable over the period for which data is available. Moreover, it is also interesting to note that the average of 14.5% in Table 2 is not far removed from the Goshen formula of 11/80 ths or 13.75%! It should, however, be made quite clear that there is no presumption that 14.5% will be the rule adopted once the Scottish Assembly is set up. The ingredient of the rule will be the subject of negotiation and discussion between the Scottish Assembly and the Westminster Parliament. Unless there is an intended disruption to Scottish public services it is unlikely that the actual ratio will, in the early years at least, diverge significantly from about 14%-15%.

This simple rule certainly satisfies the provision of allocative freedom for the Scottish Assembly but does it satisfy the other requirements of a good Grant? Is it sufficiently objective, is it 'just' and is it dynamic?

Whether or not it is objective will depend upon how well the precise rule (which is finally chosen) reflects relative needs in Scotland. In so far as expenditure-needs relationships cannot be determined precisely, there is no question of a formula-based approach being exclusively used in determining the base of a 'needs' element in the Scottish Block Fund. Moreover, if an attempt is made to tie the Grant to a needs-assessment formula then by implication this predetermines the allocation of Grant to broad categories of expenditure; although it should be realised that the final allocation is in the hands of the Assembly, who need not make the allocative decision in accordance with the needs formula.

Is the Grant system just? This is an extremely complex question to answer since it requires a careful specification of the underlying notion of distributive justice which is used. It is, however, the case that at the moment *per capita* public expenditure in Scotland is higher than *per capita* public expenditure in England even although *per capita* tax revenue raised in Scotland is lower than that raised in England. In other words, there is an element of fiscal transfer between England and Scotland in accordance with the equalization principle enunciated above. These differences are set out in Table 3.

TABLE 3

PER CAPITA PUBLIC EXPENDITURE AND TAXATION: SCOTLAND AND ENGLAND

Table 3a   Indentifiable Public Expenditure Per Capita[a]   *(£)*

	Scotland	England	(b)
1970/71	349	263	+33%
1971/72	392	296	+32%
1972/73	446	335	+33%
1973/74	492	409	+20%
1974/75	662	545	+21%
1975/76	846	691	+22%

Source: *The Economy of Scotland: A Brief Guide* (Scottish Information Office) page 3.

Notes (a) Identifiable public expenditure excludes items which cannot be appropriated between Scotland and England such as national defence.

(b) This reads for 1970/71 Scottish *per capita* public expenditure was 33% greater than that for England.

Table 3b   Per Capita Contribution of Taxation (£ per capita per annum)

	Scotland	England	Wales
1973/74	281	320	261
1974/75	364	407	334
1975/76	467	516	390

Source: Hansard, 16 November 1976, Column 511.

Note: These figures exclude revenue from local authority rates and National Insurance Contributions.

One interesting point which was raised during discussion of the
Scotland Bill in the House was an apparently sudden realisation by
many MPs, who had English constituencies, that there was such a
large difference between English and Scottish public expenditures and
between tax revenue contributions. Until now Scottish public
expenditure has not been discussed separately by Parliament. Instead,
it has been submerged in the Scottish Secretary of State's Vote for the
Scottish Office and in the Scottish Rate Support Grant etc. Now that it
is to be debated, questions about the appropriate amount of transfer
between the English regions and Scotland and thus the degree of
equalisation which is to be sought will become a highly political
question that will be fought in the open. An MP with an English
constituency, which is itself high on the scale of deprivation and
relative needs, will have to justify to his constituents why he voted in
favour of £X amount *per capita* to Scotland.

This brings us back to the question which was presented as a
paradox earlier in this chapter but which perhaps now seems like a
possible reality. Could it be that under the new financial arrangements
following the creation of the Scottish Assembly, the Scots will get less
per head by way of fiscal transfer from England than they are receiving
at the moment? This is a real possibility since it is a logical consequence
of the principle of equalization — a principle which will be openly
discussed for the first time!

One interesting feature of the equity question is that played by
housing expenditure. Public Sector Housing expenditure in Scotland
exceeds that in England. In 1975, 61% of the population in Scotland
lived in local authority housing compared with an average of 31% in
the UK. On housing subsidies alone, the average subsidy received by
all local authority households in Scotland was £290 p.a. compared to
£244 p.a. for the UK. To judge the equity of this would require that
we don't only look at direct housing expenditures and subsidies but
that we also take into account the distribution of the tax expenditures
paid out in mortgage interest reliefs. This would be a very complex
exercise but it can be seen from this argument that resolution of equity
questions will be difficult.

Finally, will the Grant be sufficiently dynamic? In other words, will
the percentage granted change with changing circumstances and
relative needs? This will depend upon how often the ratio is reviewed.
Little can be said about this *a priori*.

Having decided on some simple percentage rule to determine the
Block Grant, some people might regard this as an acceptable solution

to the problem with the only major difficulty being the initial decision upon what constitutes a just or fair percentage. But there are other features of this Grant system which are worthwhile emphasizing.

For example, whilst Scotland's Block Grant is determined as a share of equivalent English public expenditure, the actual magnitude is a function of English public expenditure which is determined by the Westminster Parliament. In this case whilst the Scottish Assembly has complete allocative freedom, the size of the Block Grant element of its budget constraint is essentially determined by Westminster. If, for example, half-way through the year the English Minister for Education produces a new programme for England which is then adopted by the Cabinet as government policy, for which additional funds are allocated, then the Scottish Block Grant would also be increased since the service (education) is a devolved function and the ratio between Scottish and English public expenditures has to be maintained. Since, however, the Scottish Assembly has allocative freedom it is not obliged to spend these additional funds on education but could instead allocate them to Scottish health services. On the other hand, however, if it was the Scottish Assembly which decided to make a marginal change to Scottish education policy there is no obvious provision made in the Bill, or elsewhere, to say how this increase in expenditure would be funded. Would it be funded out of savings on other programmes, from other revenues available to the Scottish Assembly or by negotiating a supplement to the Block Grant? If the latter course is chosen then is it not then the case that the Westminster Parliament is deciding at the margin upon Scottish policy? This assymetry in the freedom of West-minster and the Scottish Assembly to change the budget constraint part-way through the financial year is curious and should be noted. English departments appear to be able to initiate policy changes, which will activate changes in the budget constraint, but the Scottish Assembly is unable to!

The full implications of this last point are realised if we consider the consequences of a public expenditure cut. Imagine a Westminster Parliament with Conservative majority, who are intent upon reducing public expenditure, whereas there is a Labour majority in the Scottish Assembly intent upon expanding social programmes in Scotland. Since the Block Grant to the Assembly is based upon English public expenditure reductions, the latter will bring about a proportional reduction in the former.

The process of Grant negotiation and determination must by its very nature be a set of conflict relationships. It is most unlikely that the

expenditures and in the timing of public sector wage increases. The Assembly will, therefore, need to have its own public sector cost index and it could be that the independent advisory body will also monitor differences in public sector costs between Scotland and England in the event of there being a difference in interpretation between the Assembly and Westminster.

It should be clear that under conditions of inflation, like those experienced during 1973-77, the Block Grant system and the system of public expenditure control will be placed under the greatest of strains. This implies that whatever system is finally agreed upon it should be sufficiently robust to withstand the rigours of determining the Grant in conditions of rapid inflation and zero economic growth. Extreme conditions perhaps, but neverthless, conditions which have a high probability of occurring and in which the conflicts identified above will be at their most intense.

So far we have concentrated upon matters of short-run public expenditure management and control, but how will the Scottish Assembly's longer-run expenditure plans fit into the annual public expenditure White Papers and Whitehall's Public Expenditure Survey System (PESC)? The Scottish Assembly will only be asked to provide minimal information for PESC; mainly information on aggregate current and capital spending on devolved services and the Scottish public sector borrowing requirement. To get some idea of what the Scottish Assembly's entry in the public expenditure White Paper might look like, the most useful analogy is that of the Ministry of Defence's current entry. A set of forecasts of Scottish Assembly expenditure divided between capital and current account will appear and will be accompanied by a short set of explanatory notes suggesting why these figures are assumed in the forecast rather than others. There will not be a set of forecasts showing the allocation of the Grant over the various services. A mock example of what is envisaged in given in Table 4.

TABLE 4

Scottish Assembly Expenditure on Devolved Services

at 1978 Survey Prices

	1977-78 Actual Outturn	1978-79	1979-80	1980-81	1981-82	1982-83
Current Expenditure	200	210	220	230	240	250
Capital Expenditure	100	105	110	115	120	125

It is, however, interesting to consider the status of this forecast. For example, who will prepare it and on what basis will it be prepared? At the present time public expenditure forecasts are prepared upon a complex set of assumptions including views about the underlying rate of growth in productive potential, inflation, unemployment and the balance of payments. For individual public expenditure programmes it is usually assumed that the forecasts relate to the costs of unchanged policies valued at survey prices. For the forecasts of Scottish Assembly expenditure to make any sense, the Treasury will either obtain the information from the Assembly and make modifications to it or it will build it up from a 'fair shares' approach once it has forecast English equivalent expenditure.

The public expenditure forecasts could be another area in which political conflict becomes focused. In drawing up its own forecast about expenditure the Assembly will, rightly, be concerned with improving its level of service provision. It will not pay attention to the stabilization objectives of management of the overall economy. Moreover, the Assembly's forecasting system might conceivably be more accurate than the Treasury's. There is very good reason to hold this latter view. Given the size of the Assembly's budget, an integrated management of devolved services and a close working relationship with a smaller number of local authorities, the Assembly is in a strong position to produce highly sophisticated forecasts. If the Treasury's system is more crude, then errors in Treasury forecasts could be imposed upon the Grant forecast which could then at a later stage enter into Grant negotiations. Moreover, if the Treasury underforecasts Scottish Assembly expenditure, then when plans come to be implemented the Assembly may be seen to be overspending!

Nothing official has been set out about Scottish Assembly expenditure forecasting but it is clearly an area in which a number of points have to be discussed and clarified. The Scottish Assembly will have its own public expenditure forecasting unit producing forecasts and plans for Assembly decision-making. There is, therefore, nothing to stop the Assembly from publishing these forecasts. Indeed, if the forecasts do become a focus for political debate, the Assembly could publish its expenditure forecast document just before the publication of the public expenditure White Paper. If the majority parties in the Assembly and Westminster were different this could generate open debate prior to the Grant decision.

What will be the timing of the Parliamentary debate on the Assembly Block Grant? Will it come after the publication of the White Paper but

before the Budget speech, or after the Budget? The timing must be
known with certainty since it would otherwise cause havoc for financial
management within the Assembly in much the same way as universities have suffered in recent years.

How will and how should the Assembly regard the forecasts of its
expenditure which will appear in the public expenditure White Paper?
The Assembly could, for example, regard them as some kind of
guideline of Westminister's intentions for the next few years, which
will then influence its rate of development of devolved programmes.
On the other hand, it may choose to disregard the forecast and proceed
upon its own course of action. The consequences of the latter choice is
best seen by reconsidering the other sources of revenue available to the
Assembly.

Non-Grant Flow of Funds to the Assembly

It is fair to say that most of the discussion up to and during the
committee stage of the Scotland Bill concentrated upon the Block
Grant. As we saw earlier in this chapter the Grant is but one element
in the sources of funds available to the Assembly. In order to analyse
the Assembly's likely consequences to any event, such as a smaller
Grant than that anticipated, we need to pay attention to the other
elements of the budget constraint. Whilst the Assembly doesn't have
tax-raising powers, it does have the power to introduce and to make
wider use of public sector charges and pricing. For example, it could
increase local authority rents, levy prescription charges for drugs and
spectacles, raise dental charges, and introduce new charges for devolved
services. The Assembly, by withholding some grant from Scottish
local authorities, can force more local expenditure on to the local rates.
Thus, the Assembly does have an indirect means of introducing some
degree of flexibility into the budget constraint. This provokes some
important questions. Will a view of how much revenue is to be raised
from local authority rates and other charges to be taken into account
when determining the Grant? How will increases in local authority
rates and public sector charges feed back into the UK rate of inflation?
Once again, whilst these are possibilities which may emerge from the
system of financing which is proposed, we do need to assign some
notional probability of the above set of events occurring. One important
check in the system will be the reaction from the Scottish electorate
who will be asked to pay the increased local authority rates and the
new user charges. This will surely limit the probability of the Assembly
making liberal use of these other sources of finance.

Assembly-Local Government Financial Relations

The possible substitution of Block Grant revenue for local rate income does throw into relief the question of the relationships between the Scottish Assembly and Scottish local authorities post devolution day: these are dealt with in greater detail elsewhere in this book. However, as far as the financial relationships are concerned, we cannot assume that the present organisation of local government will continue. The Assembly has the power to repeal or amend the Local Government (Scotland) Acts. After devolution there will be many levels of government in Scotland: the EEC relationships, Westminster, the Scottish Assembly, local government regional and district, and community councils. It will be difficult with that number of tiers of government to keep up sufficient public interest that will ensure that they are all run with necessary vigour. It creates difficulties about the distribution of functions and responsibilities and will initially place strains on Scottish Assembly/local government relations. Additional tiers of government increase the probability of duplication and additional expense. In this situation something has to give and experience indicates that the result is usually that one of the tiers loses authority relative to the others. If the Scottish Assembly was to lose power, then devolution would be meaningless and fail and a somewhat messy unitary state would prevail. If the local tier loses, then government is removed further from the people towards a new centre. Whether or not this will threaten the spirit of devolution depends upon how much decentralisation will exist in Scotland following devolution.

Local government might, therefore, be reorganised and so too will Assembly/local government financial relationships. Despite the precise form which any new structure might take, the Assembly will provide grant in aid finance to the Scottish local governments and will depend upon good relationships with the local authorities for service delivery and in providing information to the Assembly on local conditions. The Assembly could, in the course of time, decide to give the Scottish local governments financial assistance in a different way. For example, it might decide to make more extensive use of specific Grants rather than the present general Block Grant of RSG. However, in the early years prior to any such changes, the current system will prevail with the Assembly's 'Secretary for Finance' negotiating RSG with the representatives of COSLA (Convention of Scottish Local Authorities). Since Scottish local authorities will also receive funds from the Secretary of State for Scotland for reserved functions, COSLA will also negotiate with the Scottish Office directly.

Regional Development and Growth

One of the controversial omissions from the Scotland Bill is the non-devolution of responsibility to the Assembly for regional and industrial policy in Scotland. Whilst it is clear that the pace of economic activity within Scotland depends upon events which take place outside of that economy, the relatively poor performance of the Scottish economy, measured primarily in terms of its relative level of unemployment, has been a source of discontent and has generated demands for greater devolved responsibility for industrial policy. The appropriate degree of devolution in this sphere has been resolved with the passing of the Scotland Bill and will continue to be a focus for major debate in the future.

It has already been argued in this chapter that the Scottish Assembly's policies will be unable to make significant contributions to changes in aggregate demand. That is, monetary and fiscal policies are not feasible policy instruments available to the Assembly to influence the level of Scottish employment. Policies to reduce the *long-term* or structural level of unemployed are, in any case, not matters of demand management but are instead questions of adjusting the supply side of the economy. That is why an appropriate and regional policy could be of such importance to the performance of the Scottish economy and, therefore, why there has been disappointment with the provisions which have been made in the Scotland Act.

In order to separate out the arguments of this part of the debate we will consider the present set-up with respect to regional and industrial policy in Scotland, the provisions made in the Scotland Act, and an alternative arrangement.

(a) At present, in Scotland, industrial and regional policy is exercised through the instruments of the Scottish Development Agency (SDA), central government 'rescue operations', the various planning functions of local government and the Highlands and Islands Development Board (HIDB). Both the SDA and the HIDB are *ad hoc* bodies. Section 2(2) of the Scottish Development Agency Act 1975 sets out the Agency's functions, which are essentially to promote the growth and modernisation of industry in Scotland by providing/assisting with the provision of finance or other resources. In 1976-77 the SDA expected to commit £15m to investment, £22m to factory sites and buildings and £14m to land renewal. The SDA is expected to meet objectives of commercial viability and profitability in its assistance operations.

(b)   The functions of the SDA, after devolution, will be roughly maintained as now and will be circumscribed by guidelines under subsection 1(a) of Section 42 of the Scotland Act. These guidelines will cover matters such as target rates of return, minimum interest rates on loans made by the Agency, and circumstances in which the Agency can make grants. The powers under Section 5 of the SDA Act, which permit the Secretary of State to exercise his powers of selective financial assistance under Section 7 of the 1972 Industry Act, are reserved. The environmental and derelict land functions of the Agency are now devolved. Like the SDA the HIDB's economic development functions are reserved under the Scotland Act and are subject to guidelines. This does not, however, apply to HIDB's social development function.

Thus whilst Schedule II of the Act transfers to the Executive certain functions in relation to the SDA and HIDB, the Government will remain generally responsible for regional and industrial policy in Scotland. It does this by transmitting guidelines for these SDA and HIDB functions and obliges the Executive to use its powers in such a way as to give effect to the guidelines. The implementation of the guidelines and the enforcement of the resulting directions are thus the responsibility of the Executive but the Government will have reserve powers to ensure that the guidelines are observed.

(c)   An alternative proposal would be to devolve completely to the Assembly the powers of deciding upon industrial and regional policies i.e., devolve responsibility for setting the guidelines. The activities of the SDA and the HIDB would then be financed out of the Block Grant, thereby giving the Assembly an opportunity to discuss how much to allocate to industrial and regional policy in accordance with its perception of priorities. In Northern Ireland, as in most other federal countries, powers over regional and industrial development are devolved.

One argument in favour of devolving such powers to the Assembly is that decisions could be made more quickly. There are many instances in which companies planning to locate factories in Scotland have ultimately located elsewhere than in the UK because of delays in gaining planning permission etc. Because everything is referred to the Treasury it can take up to nine months to receive a decision. Another argument is that a Scottish Assembly could tailor regional policy to Scottish needs rather than having such policies centralised in London. There is also the potential for a more flexible and innovative policy of regeneration and restructuring of industry rather than the traditional employment subsidies which have been used in the past and which maintain the existing industrial structure.

The predominant argument which was moved against the devolution of industrial policy was that a Scottish freedom to decide upon guidelines for the SDA would introduce 'unfair' distortions and would undermine the efficiency of UK regional policy. This argument is, however, based upon a curious logic which assumes that current regional policy is efficient; this flies in the face of the facts. Surely the whole idea of regional and industrial incentives is to introduce differentials? If regulated competition amongst various regions promotes a more vigorous industrial base then is that not to be encouraged? A more imaginative set of policies from a Scottish Assembly could induce Westminster to adopt similar policies!

It should, however, be noted that there is nothing in the Scotland Bill to prevent the Assembly setting up something like a Scottish Economic Department Council to provide differential regional incentives financed out of the Block Grant. However, much of the success of regional policy will depend upon the Assemblymen's knowledge of the working of industry and commerce and on how well informed they are by their bureaucracy.

Alongside any potential benefits arising from the Assembly's differential industrial/regional policies must be laid the costs to industry of having to deal with another layer of government. These are costs arising from compliance and cosultation in an environment of complex government/business relationships. Could, for example, small businesses afford this? Would it not be more sensible for the Assembly to be responsible for this function? The debate will undoubtedly continue.

Pay Policy

A curious anomaly in the Bill arises in connection with pay policy. It is not at all clear if the Assembly can be held to observe UK Government pay policy (see Hansard, 10 January 1978, Col. 1592 and House of Lords debate Vol. 391, No. 71, Col. 228). If the Assembly is required to conform to such policies then it loses a degree of freedom in determining its own policy with respect to the management of the devolved services. For example, if something like a firemen's strike took place both in Scotland and England and if the Assembly settled with the firemen outside the terms of the UK Government's pay code then would not this have serious consequences for the UK Government's public sector pay policy in particular, and for its wider pay policy generally? One means of improving devolved services in Scotland would be to attract certain groups of public sector workers into these services by paying them more than their English counterparts, thereby closing manpower gaps. The extent to which such a policy might be persued by the Assembly will obviously be constrained by the availability of finance.

Clearly this is an ill-defined area and an area of potential conflict. Whether or not the UK Government will exercise threats to the Assembly, e.g., that it will cut its Grant unless it conforms on pay policy, remains to be seen. But on something like a voluntary incomes policy it is not at all obvious what powers would be available to the UK Government in this respect other than the power of persuasion.

The Assembly and Tax-Raising Powers

Finally there is the major unresolved question of whether or not the Assembly should have its own independent tax-raising powers. Undoubtedly this issue will continue to be debated for some considerable amount of time to come. It must be admitted that the Goverment's discussion documents on this topic which preceeded the formulation of the Scotland Bill failed to convince any serious-minded student of fiscal federalism that it was either impossible, administratively or technically, or indeed undesirable to grant tax-raising powers to the Assembly. It would take too long, and, moreover, would be inappropraite in this essay to work systematically through this debate but it is nevertheless worthwhile making the following points.

Independent tax-raising powers or tax revenue sharing are characteristic of all federal countries. There is no clear reason why this cannot also be so for a semi-federal country like the proposed UK set-up. Granting the Scots access to some part of the tax base will not be destabilizing and will not frustrate the Treasury's macro-economic policy. Currently about £1200m is raised via income tax in Scotland. If the Assembly was to vary this amount by plus or minus 20% (a significant amount!) this would either raise or lower the figure by £400m. Sir Douglas Wass of the Treasury has, however, stated that ± £1,000m will not affect Treasury demand management, so how could the taxation decisions of the Assembly? (See Hansard, 10 January 1978, Col. 1531).

Conclusions

Some would argue that the financial arrangements in the Bill constitute the most serious source of instability in the new pattern of government in Scotland. Whilst there is the potential for much conflict between the Scottish Assembly and Westminster we have, in this chapter, tried to balance this view by considering the checks within the system which might resolve or at least temper any conflict. Whether or not the financial provisions in the Bill will aid the workability of devolution remains to be seen. Certainly there is no other country in the world which has an executive and a legislative body which does not have tax-raising powers: in this sense the Assembly has less formal power than local government!

Chapter 9

The Policy Process

JAMES G. KELLAS

ATTENTION generally focuses on the Scottish Assembly when devolution is discussed. This is only to be expected, since the Assembly is the source of legitimacy for the new Scottish Government, and most clauses of the Scotland Act relate to the powers of the Assembly, directly or indirectly. The Scottish Government, or Executive, must have the confidence of the Assembly, although with fixed terms of four years, this will not be exactly as at Westminster. Only when two-thirds of the total number of Assembly members concur can a dissolution take place. This will produce a somewhat more independent and 'separate' role for the legislative and executive branches of government, and tend to weaken party discipline, since the fate of the Government is not closely tied to votes in the legislature. While this may strengthen the legislative branch, it could also make the Executive less interested in Assembly affairs. This has happened in France, under somewhat similar arrangements.

Devolution provides the Assembly with legislative powers which it alone may exercise, except on the rare occasions when Parliament decides to override Assembly Bills, or to legislate itself in devolved matters. It is the clear intention of the Scotland Bill to draw a line somewhere between devolved and non-devolved matters. Should that line be in doubt, there is recourse to judicial interpretation. This method of operation is part of the British tradition in devolution, since under the Stormont system certain powers were 'transferred' to the Northern Ireland Parliament. Thus the Assembly might expect to be able to go about 'its business' (i.e., legislation in devolved matters) without interference from Parliament, either through the use of override powers, or through the concurrent power of legislation in devolved matters. This makes the Assembly the master in its own house, and not linked into the operations of Parliament.

However, legislation is only one activity of government, and one that is dependent on the managerial function. The managerial function means the provision of resources, both financial and administrative, for government, and the formulation and control of policy. In these respects, the Assembly is clearly replaced by the Scottish Executive, just as in British Government Whitehall and Downing Street have very separate identities and functions from those of the Palace of Westminster (Parliament). In the UK system of government, the Cabinet is responsible for the legislative programme, the management of the economy, and the administration of central and (more loosely) local government. It is of course served by the whole apparatus of Government departments and agencies, including ministers, Civil Servants, and appointees of various kinds. The relationship of the 'executive branch' to the 'legislative branch' is one of the most difficult in constitutional analysis, but as far as the UK is concerned most would agree that the centre of decision-making is in Whitehall, not Westminster.

Will Scottish devolution provide a completely different balance of power as between the legislature and the executive? Probably not, and here I differ from John Mackintosh in chapter 4. Although the Assembly may well be a more powerful legislative body than Parliament in some respects, especially if it develops a system of specialised committees which can probe the activities of Scottish departments and share to some extent in policy-making, it is fatally weakened by the peculiar constitutional position of the Scottish Executive. For that Executive is not only strong in relation to the Assembly, but extremely dependent on its relations with the UK Government. The result is that while the Scottish Executive has to pursue its managerial role in devolved matters (formulating expenditure proposals and framing legislation to put the Assembly), it in turn is subject to the managerial role of the UK Government. While the UK Government does not seek to manage devolved matters as such, it controls them indirectly, through the Block Grant, since that is directly related to the expenditure proposals of the Scottish Executive. Whether the Block Grant is built up on the basis of 'needs' measured against comparable needs in England, the Scottish Executive is likely to be faced with accepting UK Government priorities, or risking a breakdown of Grant negotiations. Moreover, the Grant will not be paid out in a lump sum for the financial year, but in stages. This gives the Treasury futher controls over any 'misspending' by the Scottish Executive.

The alternatives to this close control of the Scottish Government by the UK Government are to change the formula for the Block Grant so that a fixed sum comes to Scotland as of right (i.e., irrespective of an assessment of 'needs' by the UK Government), or to provide the Assembly with its own revenue-raising (i.e., tax) powers, so that it can finance its own needs as it sees them. A well-known hybrid between a needs-based Block Grant and an unconditional Grant or shared revenue, is the 'conditional grant' found in federal countries. This allows the central (here, the UK) government to introduce a programme and determine the categories of need which will benefit from it, but allows the subnational (Scottish) government to adopt it voluntarily, and to alter it within limits to suit its own priorities. However, the Scotland Act has not used this device, nor the fixed-formula devolved revenue, and so the Scottish Executive is tied very closely to the priorities determined by the UK Government.

These are not the only ties binding the Scottish Executive to the UK Government. The UK keeps *legislative* powers in matters which are nevertheless to be *administered* by the Scottish Executive (Schedule 11). There is thus a mis-match between the legislative and executive powers to be devolved, and in an odd way the Scottish Executive is here found executing laws passed by Parliament, and not by its own Assembly. The principal areas involved are land use and development (a very sensitive area in Scottish politics), pollution, and road traffic.

Moreover, the Secretary of State for Scotland (a UK Cabinet minister) functions often in a tutelary or overlord capacity with regard to the Executive (his powers over the Assembly are more ceremonial, along the lines of a 'Governor-General'). The numerous references to the Secretary of State in the Scotland Act show that the Executive is not master of its own house in many respects, while the Assembly can hope to legislate freely in devolved matters. For example, the whole area of planning is complicated by the continuation of powers of the Secretary of State to intervene and take over the proceedings in certain circumstances (Schedule 14). This will necessitate a duplication of expert planning staff in the Scottish Office (new style) and in the Scottish Executive. Then there are the 'Scheduled Functions' of local government, such as police, careers service, and offices, shops and railway premises. It is easy to see how problems of co-ordination could arise between these 'non-devolved' UK services of local government, linked to the Scottish Office and the devolved ones of crime, education and land use linked to the Scottish Executive. What is clear is that the Scottish Executive will be constantly looking over its shoulder to the Scottish Office and to the UK Government generally, for fear of missing some 'guidelines' or consent powers in its own sphere, or because a vital function in a related field is in fact still part of the UK administration.

As it can in relation to local government, the UK Government can step in to force the Scottish Executive to act, or to stop acting, if it considers that it is transgressing into a reserved matter, including European Community matters or international obligations. This shows again how closely linked the Scottish Executive is with the UK Government, and how subordinate it is in that respect. To make matters more certain for the UK all the Civil Servants working for the Scottish Government are members of the UK Civil Service, responsible to the Civil Service Department and the Prime Minister as minister for the Civil Service.

This points to a general conclusion about the Scottish Executive. It stands somewhat detached from the Assembly through the 'fixed term' provision, and through the normal separation of the executive branch of government from the legislature in nearly every country. As elsewhere, it must perform the managerial function of initiating policy and administering government. No Assembly, however powerful, can take on these functions.

Yet there is, as we have seen, something quite extraordinary about the Scottish Executive in its relation to the UK Government. Its dependence on that Government is so close that one is almost tempted to describe it as a branch of the UK Government itself, although certainly not an equal partner. Its daily workings can only be successful if it succeeds in persuading the UK Government to supply it with funds, to under-write its priorities, and to actually administer its affairs. This amounts to an 'interpenetration' of the subnational government by the central government to an extent unknown in federal systems, or even in the devolved system of government in Northern Ireland from 1921 to 1972. For Stormont had its own Civil Service and did not operate on a Block Grant.

How can one explain this peculiar situation, and how is it going to work in practice? First, it must be noted that politicians have always known the distinction between 'devolution to an Assembly' and 'devolution to an Assembly and a Government'. In the former case, there is only a 'debating-chamber' or a legislative body which acts under the control of the UK Government, as does Parliament (normally). Policy, legislative proposals, and the management of affairs remain in the hands of the UK Government. Thus, the Conservative Party favoured a weak form of devolution which gave Scotland an Assembly but not a Government. In that way 'the Crown' would still be the only government in Scotland, and the Assembly would have to work with and under the control of the UK Government. The Labour

change in the financing of devolution, from the Block Grant to a fixed formula and a revenue-raising power. It also means freeing Scottish priorities from these shaped in Whitehall. It leads to the merging of the Scottish Office, Lord Advocate's Department, etc., functions with those of the Scottish Executive, and the establishment of a separate Scottish Civil Service. These things will not happen immediately, but the success of devolution ultimately depends on them.

Chapter 10

The Administrative Process

JAMES MCGUINNESS

CHAPTER 9 has outlined some of the major problems likely to emerge from the attempt to interrelate the policy and managerial functions of the Scottish Executive on the one hand, and the legislative and other functions of the Scottish Assembly on the other. It is not the expectation of the present contributor that, at this stage of the process, one can do more than sketch some possible lines of approach towards a solution of these difficulties. To adapt a Churchillian formula, the Royal Assent to the devolution legislation is not even the end of the beginning; and it seems doubtful whether even the draftsmen and the dedicated navigators of the Bill through the House fully realise how many 'grey areas' between the 'devolved' administrations in Edinburgh on the one hand and the Scottish Office (new style) and the rump departments therein on the other, have still to be delimited.

Let us first clear a little of the ground on terminology, especially for readers who may not have had the time, appetite or stamina to digest the content of the Scotland Act. In fact, obfuscation by terminology starting from the semantics of the term 'devolution' itself (not defined in the Act except in terms of the matters said to be 'devolved') has been one of the characteristic features of debate both inside and outside Parliament since the Kilbrandon Commission reported. In this contribution, an attempt will be made to avoid using the terms Scottish Executive, First Secretary and Scottish Secretaries, hallowed though they may be by the Act itself. The non-professional reader will find these terms confusing and indeed unprecedented in any political context. Instead, where we can, we will talk about the 'First Minister' and 'Scottish departmental ministers' and the 'Scottish departments', where we are referring to those instruments of administration based in Edinburgh and concerned mainly with devolved functions: and confine the term Secretary to the Secretary of State for Scotland himself in relation to those functions retained by him and by his department, based partly in Edinburgh and partly in London, which we will call the Scottish Office. A more coherent and intelligible nomenclature will probably be devised — or rather emerge — in due course; but these terminological obscurities, like so many others in this legislation, must be left to be clarified *ambulando*, so to speak.

As every Scottish schoolboy knows, or should know, there are at present five major Scottish departments based on, and operating from, Edinburgh. They are the Departments of Home and Health; Education; Agriculture and Fisheries; Development; and Economic Planning. At present these are all departments of the Scottish Office, whose chief official is styled (in the archaic language the British Civil Service inherited from the French) the Permanent Under-Secretary of State.

It is simplest perhaps to begin at the very top and pose a direct question at this point. In the new structure, who in fact will be Scotland's top Civil Servant? In brief, what will the relationship be between the Permanent Under-Secretary of State at the Scottish Office (new style) and the most senior head of the most senior department in the Scottish departments serving Scotland's First Minister and his colleagues in the Scottish 'Cabinet'? Some reflections on this are given later; but let it suffice meantime to put the question; the ultimate answer to it may help to illustrate perhaps more clearly than any other where effective power and authority will really reside in the remodelled system of professional administration.

Before attempting to answer this question, it seems essential to look more closely at the probable reconstruction of the Scottish departments which will form part of the new Scottish devolved administration. Much more is entailed than the straightforward realignment of the existing departments as they stand: for example, it would be wrong to assume that these departments will simply acquire ministerial heads, responsible to the Assembly, and will perform all their 'Parliamentary' work in relation to the Assembly and not to Westminster without further changes being needed.

The British system of public administration is based on three main centres of ministerial and bureaucratic authority and power. The Treasury, of which the Prime Minister is still First Lord, and which until 1968 was also responsible for the Civil Service, the Cabinet Office, and the Foreign Office, which although an integral part of our Civil Service has always been in a distinctive position. All these departments enjoy quite special influence, power and authority, in the British system of government; and it is arguable that whatever

theoretical demerits this concentration of authority may have, in the
British context it was historically and politically inevitable.

The new devolved Scottish administration (political and administrative) will need to have a corresponding, if much less significant, power
base. It would be naive to think that such a base could be any other
than the office of the First Minister (First Secretary in the Act) since it
is he who is responsible for advising the Secretary of State (in the
latter's quasi-Governor-General capacity) on which members of the
Assembly should be appointed to ministerial office. Moreover, it is he
who is ultimately accountable to the Assembly for its administration.

It would be most natural in these circumstances that one of the first
measures to be taken by the new First Minister and his colleagues
would be to create an office for the management and conduct of their
affairs — a Scottish Cabinet Office in effect if not in name. This Office,
which like the British Cabinet Office would be *de facto* part of the
First Minister's equivalent of 'No. 10' (Downing Street, as an office
rather than a residence), would be responsible for the co-ordination of
the legislative and other programmes of the Assembly (in co-operation
and consultation with the Assembly's own officials).

It is difficult at this stage to predict whether it is likely, or indeed
desirable, that the First Minister's Office viz the Scottish 'Cabinet'
Office could or should wield similar authority and exercise the same
co-ordinating role as the Cabinet Office in Whitehall: or indeed
whether the chief official in the Scottish administration should be the
Secretary of the Cabinet. Much must depend on the role of the Scottish
Minister and his department charged with the preparation and
co-ordination and negotiation (briefed by the Finance Department and
through the Scottish Office) of the Block Grant. Indeed this key
responsibility might well be assumed by the First Minister himself.

Ultimately such decisions must be taken, or at least approved, by
the Assembly itself; but the Assembly cannot even begin to function
until some central administration, however modest, is at the disposal
of the First Minister.

Initially other ministers should be able to operate immediately with
the support of the existing St Andrews House departments, since there
are no devolved functions which are not already being handled by
skilled and experienced officials in those departments.

Broadly speaking, one can invisage a ministerial and departmental
structure, based on the existing Scottish Office departments, as
follows:

Minister	*Departments*
First Minister (possibly also holding the portfolio of Finance)	Cabinet Office + Finance and Establishments (At present 2 divisions of the Scottish Office)
Land Use (including land management) Physical Planning Environment	Scottish Development Department (part) Department of Agriculture (part)
Housing and Local Government Services (except Roads, Police and Fire Services)	Scottish Development Department (part)
Transport and Roads Tourism New Towns Scottish Development Agency Highlands and Islands Development Board	Scottish Economic Planning Department (part)
Education, Social Work Services, the Arts, and Recreation	Scottish Education Department
Health Services and Home Affairs (including Police and Fire Services)	Scottish Home and Health Department

Initially this would give a Scottish Cabinet of 6 ministers with Under-Secretaries (or Deputies) in the major departments where there were clearly separate groups of functions. (The Lord Advocate's Department and the Crown Office are *sui generis* and their functions are discussed in chapter 10).

The recruitment, conditions of service, and remuneration of officials in these departments are not, at least initially, affected by the Act. It provides quite simply that officials of the Scottish departments will be employed 'in Her Majesty's Home Civil Service, and appointments shall be made accordingly.' (Section 67(1)). On the other hand, the Act also empowers Scottish ministers to appoint such officers as they 'may think appropriate' for the exercise of their powers. It would therefore be odd indeed if appointments to the Scottish departments had for all time to be made only by, or only as authorised by, the Civil Service department in Whitehall — which is what the last few words of Section 67(1) theoretically require.

In practical terms the present St Andrews House departments (or rather the Scottish Office, since Personnel Management is now a centralised service for all the Scottish departments) already enjoy a significant measure of autonomy in the selection and promotion of staff; although in the higher reaches, the influence and indirectly expressed judgments of the Civil Service department and Treasury are important; indeed, under the present regime, essential. Currently, the appointment of the Permanent Under-Secretary of State, Scottish Office, and of his deputies (the Secretaries of the Scottish departments) requires the approval of the Prime Minister. It is not clear whether the appointment of heads of departments serving Scottish ministers in Edinburgh will still require similar approval, or the approval of the Secretary of State for Scotland. The Northern Ireland administration prior to direct rule provides no guidance here: the Northern Ireland Civil Service was completely separate and independent of Whitehall.

It might be argued that such formal approvals of very senior officials are integral to the unity of the Home Civil Service and essential to the maintenance of appropriate standards — in particular the relative competence of performance as between the heads of the Scottish departments (new style) and the most senior officials in the Scottish Office. Indeed the Civil Servants themselves may well wish to have common seniority lists for both the Scottish departments and the Scottish Office and common standards of assessment of performance as prescribed by the Civil Service department.

On the other hand, it seems scarcely credible that any First Minister in Scotland could for long defend a position in which all the appointments of all the chief officials in his administration required the formal approval of the Secretary of State or even the Prime Minister. The Scottish Assembly for their part are bound to resent a situation in which they and the Executive would have less freedom in this respect than even the smallest local authority. It seems likely therefore that, while much may be achieved initially by consultation between the First Minister and the Secretary of State about appointments to the Scottish departments, the emergence of a separate Civil Service with a separate career structure will come to be regarded as inevitable.

It is to be expected that if the new Scottish system of devolved government is to draw upon, as well as to be open to, 'all the talents', it will draw freely from the outset on expertise in the devolved subjects available outside the Civil Service and will develop the flexibility already secured by the Scottish Office in making both temporary, *ad hoc* and permanent appointments of experts in specific fields from the universities and elsewhere. It has to be kept in mind, on the other hand, that however keen the new First Minister and his ministerial team may be to develop new initiatives, new ideas and new men, the inhibitions will be formidable. 'Parity' and 'the rate for the job' have become accepted, indeed paramount, concepts in all matters of personnel management; apart altogether from the power wielded by the Civil Service Unions.

It would therefore be an enormous task to develop in anything less than a decade a totally new approach to government service and management, especially in the field of creative ideas and initiatives, and in managerial competence. Many people feel that it is these capacities above all which are lacking in the British Civil Service as a whole and that the over-intellectualised analytical approach to public administration is one of a complex of reasons why nationally we have fallen so far behind our competitors.

It would be fundamentally wrong, on the other hand, to be pessimistic about the possibilities open to the new Scottish administration; but it is impossible for Scotland to expect always to have the bread buttered on both sides . If the Civil Service is to be encouraged to be constructive, imaginative, and even daring in its thinking within the devolved fields, it will have to persuade (or as the French 'Civil Servants' say, *convaincre*) Scottish ministers and the Assembly that whether the English and Welsh are getting away with something that costs 'more' or 'less' is irrelevant. The real question is whether a better result can be achieved appropriate to Scottish conditions with fairly allocated resources. Ministers and the Assembly must equally have the courage to support the administration once they have been 'convinced'. These questions of intitiatives and ideas; competence in performance and in management of resources are the crux of administration in a complex modern society. The slight 'touch of the tiller', negative, relatively fail-safe, amateur type of bureaucracy is simply archaic in our day and age. This point has been laboured, because in the past the popularly accepted political theory that ministers alone both initiate and make policy and that Civil Servants merely carry it out is to some degree an illusion or half-truth (fostered in part by the Civil Service itself and strengthened a great deal, let it be said, by the 'Manifesto' politics of recent years). Half-truth though it may be, it tends in its oversimplification to create much misunderstanding of the proper role of the Civil Service, and puts a premium on waiting for the file 'to come down with the problems' rather than 'on putting it up with the ideas'.

This digression is felt to be important, because in some fields of Scottish administration very many policy initiatives start in Whitehall and are then 'supported' and 'adopted' either simply or with qualifications by the Scottish department concerned. This is inevitably the case where the initiative represents the application of a manifesto or other promulgated party political commitment which the Government of the day have decided to honour. But these are not the sole initiatives: there may well be others started by the 'English' Minister or by his officials. It is relatively rare for initiatives to be taken in Scotland, to survive intact through interdepartmental discussion in Whitehall, to emerge from the elaborate network of official committees supervised by the Cabinet Office, Treasury, or department principally involved, and to be ultimately endorsed by the Cabinet.

Of course, there have been very many notable exceptions, for example, in social work services, regional and Highland development, agriculture advisory services and other fields, but the general proposition holds good. It take a very energetic tail to wag a large dog which may not quite know where it wants to go! One of the major tasks therefore of all Scottish departments has been to find out early enough what their opposite numbers in Whitehall are up to; and to make certain that the Scottish interest is not only fully taken into account but substantially safeguarded and developed. If not, the Secretary of State will personally intervene with the appropriate minister and Cabinet committee or even directly with the Prime Minister. But what is to be the future of this elaborate process of intercommunion and vigilant intelligence work under the new structure of devolved government? The almost personal links and interlocutions will of course continue; but personalities and policies change. The British Civil Service notoriously moves people around in a manner which quite bewilders our European and Transatlantic friends — and it will not be very long before the Scottish departments will be 'out on their own' so to speak, except for such general liaison as can be maintained with the Whitehall machine through the Scottish Office (new style) and the Secretary of State.

The role of that Office will indeed be crucial to the success of the devolutionary experiment. It will be finally responsibile for negotiating (and monitoring) the Assembly Block Grant; for administering and protecting the Scottish interest in all the retained functions; and for maintaining effective liaison with UK departments operating in Scotland, some of whose functions are of vital significance to the Scottish economy, e.g., Energy, Defence, Employment, Industry, Trade and others. It will of course comprehend those departments whose functions are not devolved (in particular major sections of the Scottish Economic Planning Department, the Department of Agriculture and Fisheries and Forestry) but it seems likely that its main role will have to be an increasing involvement in the problems and potential of the Scottish economy.

There is one obvious reason why this is inevitable. Scottish members of the Westminster Parliament will no longer be entitled to intervene directly at question time, in debate, or in correspondence with the Scottish Office in such matters as housing, education, and other 'devolved' services which have in the past bulked so largely in their constituency post-bags and 'surgeries'. They will therefore not only have more time but will be expected to use it in bending their energies to tackling issues which are of great importance but which Parliament has decided Scottish ministers and the Assembly cannot control. The most important are industry and employment and energy and the economy generally, (including prices and incomes) and the social security services. In the rural constituencies particularly, agricultural policy and fishing and forestry will continue to be dominant issues. Except in the last group the Secretary of State has few, if any, executive functions but is none the less expected to express in Cabinet and elsewhere the Scottish view and defend the Scottish interest.

But his involvement and exposure to attack will be greatest in the process of determination of the Block Grant. His department (the Scottish Office — new style) will have to assume responsibility for the detailed negotiations with the Treasury and through the Public Expenditure Survey Committee, without having direct executive responsibility for the services financed from the Block Grant. The Scottish Office, with its centralised Finance Department, already contains experienced officials who can participate and indeed take a strong lead in this respect, but in future it will not be able to proceed without almost a complete 'in house' rapport with the financial officials in the Scottish departments who will be estimating their requirements and accounting both to the Assembly and to the Scottish Office and Treasury for what they spend. It is here that the field of potential administrative intricacy and political ambiguity is almost completely uncharted. What most officials would expect is that given the background, experience and provenance of those concerned, the relationship would initially be at least as good as that prevailing between the Scottish Office and local government officials in the formulation and distribution of the local Government grant. Indeed, it would be natural for the new Scottish

Ministry of Finance to draw a proportion of its staff from the Scottish Office. But the officials of the Scottish departments will both collectively and individually be more exposed, especially if the Assembly decides to create a complex committee system. Much more important therefore even than their relationship with the Scottish Office will be their relationship with one another and with their own Department of Finance. The whole theory of the Block Grant is that it will give the Scottish administration and the Assembly some scope for flexibility in allocating funds between the devolved services. But the line between amicably agreed flexibility and anarchic interdepartmental squabbling is hard to draw and the Whitehall machine achieves it largely by a rigorous Treasury control which it would be regrettable to have to reproduce in Scotland. There is an assumption in public debate on this subject that flexibility in allocating expenditure to devolved services can really be left to — indeed should be a prime function of — the Assembly itself; but this is the kind of political truism which makes plausible constitutional theory but impractical administration. The Scottish Cabinet, on the advice of the Scottish departments must put their 'budget' to the Assembly and its relevant committees and then let it be examined and voted upon in the usual way. It becomes obvious then that within the Scottish administration for the devolved services, there must be co-ordinated machinery for framing the expenditure programmes of the separate departments; that this machinery must in the initial stages be managed by the Scottish Department of Finance (as at Stormont), with the Scottish Cabinet Secretariat holding a watching brief, so that when the proposals go forward to the First Minister and the Cabinet, there can be a smoother path to a co-ordinated presentation to the Assembly or to the appropriate Assembly committee in the first instance.

The administrative and other processes of preparing budgetary fore- casts of public expenditure on the devolved services are examined elsewhere in this book (chapter 8). The main purpose of the previous paragraphs (which in part represent a digression from our main theme) is to try to bring into general focus the respective roles of the Scottish departments (new style) on the one hand and the Scottish Office (new style) on the other.

We have however so far only touched the fringe of a difficult, in some respects intractable, problem of interdepartmental communica- tion. Within the Scottish departments the difficulties should be surmountable. The leading officials are well known to one another, they are loyal to Scotland, and those who decide to stay in the

Edinburgh administration will be committed to making the new system work. With proper leadership both within the service and particularly from their own 'top Civil Servant', as yet unidentified, and with full backing from the First Minister and his colleagues and from the Assembly, they should be able to develop an efficient machine.

The position of the Scottish Office (new style) seems more doubtful. In some respects their task seems more formidable. If the assumption that they and their Secretary of State will be open to attack on two main fronts — the state of the Scottish economy and the 'inadequacy' of the Block Grant is accurate, then it is more important than ever that they should wield weight and influence in the Whitehall machine — in committee, in private interdepartmental debate and argument about all aspects of economic policy, our relationships with Europe, and in many other fields. The more successes they have in these matters the more credible and effective they are likely to be on the other field of greater difficulty — the fight over the Block Grant. But to achieve this degree of strength requires a substantial re-examination both of the Secretary of State's own role and participation in Cabinet committees (it has been argued that he is not a member of certain key committees whose work and decisions are critical to the Scottish economy) and of Scottish officials in the major official Whitehall groups and committees. The fact that the Scotland Act gives certain 'paramount chief' powers to the Secretary of State in relation to the Scottish First Minister and his colleagues and the Scottish departments (new style) will be regarded in Whitehall as of relatively slight 'regional' interest now that the legislation is enacted. These powers will not of themselves give the Secretary of State and his Scottish Office (new style) the political and administrative authority to sustain his new role unless at the same time his own (and his department's) formal participation in the Whitehall machine is more firmly secured.

It follows that the official standing and influence of the Scottish Office (new style) must not be diminished by these changes. In particular, the status of the Permanent Under-Secretary of State and his deputies (heading the non-devolved departments of that office) must be maintained and they or their representatives must have much fuller representation in all relevant Whitehall committee and other machinery, concerned not only with the non-devolved functions and with the management of the economy but also with our growing relationship with Europe.

Perhaps we can now attempt to answer the question. Let us have two top Civil Servants — one in Edinburgh (the Permanent Under-Secretary

or Chief Executive in the Department of the First Minister (and
Minister of Finance) and the Permanent Under-Secretary of State,
Scottish Office (new style) both equally remunerated, equally respected,
and equally competent; let them meet at least once a week (in term
time!) and not just twice a year to discuss their respective administrations' recommendations of names for inclusion in the Birthday and
New Year Honours Lists! To observe the proprieties of balance and
equilibrium, let them (like their peers in Whitehall) meet alternately at
one another's offices (or lunch tables). They might even be invited
alternately to the weekly meetings of Permanent Secretaries in
Whitehall — but this could be asking too much. Where do the Welsh
and the Northern Irish (if devolution is ever restored to that sorely
tried Province) come in?

Chapter 11

Local Government and the Scottish Assembly

STUART PAGE

A VIEW on the future of Scottish local government after the coming into effect of the Scottish Assembly depends upon the assessment of a variety of factors, and notably of the methods adopted by the Assembly in the conduct of its own affairs. Other key issues include the formal impact of the Act, and the freedom further to modify the areas, status, functions and financing of local government. At the same time, the possible effects of the Assembly on local government are a matter to be kept in mind in setting up the internal organisation of the Assembly, since, in the new circumstances, the Assembly and Scottish local government must have a close relationship at all levels of activity.

Implied in what follows in this paper is the fundamental assumption that a vigorous and flourishing local government, based upon local policy-making by democratically elected bodies, is in the best interests of Scotland, and that a prime objective of the Assembly will be to preserve this and encourage and support it in every way.

The immediate effect of the Act on local government is neutral. The references are brief, and on the surface appear to be mainly technical. The matters devolved to the Assembly and the Scottish Secretary are particularised, and are expressed in highly legalistic form, and the reserved (or scheduled) functions of local authorities are listed. The Act permits the Assembly to modify the system of local rates, or allow substitute taxes of the same nature. The Scottish Secretary is able to enter into agency arrangements with other authorities, including local authorities, on a very flexible basis, and this facility could open new doors for local government, given the necessary political will. The settlement of the problems which these important but mainly technical and procedural matters must undoubtedly raise can be organised in the traditional and well-tried manner, but even these may have unsuspected consequences for the relationships between the Assembly and local government.

The major effect of the emergence of the Assembly on local government will be the injection into the public decision-making machinery of a new and additional level of government. The unsatisfied demands for a further look at the reformed system of local government have been increasingly coupled with the prospective activities of the Assembly, the latter being seen as the lever to be used to redraw the areas of local authorities and re-allocate the functions within the total framework of government. Despite the intensive studies undertaken by the Royal Commission on Local Government in Scotland, and the inherent logic in many of the Wheatley recommendations, the Commission's prescription for reform, which was adopted in substance by Parliament, was not universally acceptable. It is not unreasonable to predict that an early task urged upon the Assembly will be a fresh and probably hasty search for a new formula for the local government structure and for new relationships with central government, the Assembly taking on the most of the role of the Scottish Office in all its aspects and ramifications.

The possibilities for change depend partly upon the alleged defects of the post-1975 local government system. The financial aspects of local government in relation to the Assembly are examined elsewhere in this book, but a brief reference at this point is necessary. The arguments about the proper balance between the central and the local contributions to local government were ably and exhaustively presented in the Layfield Report on Local Government Finance, and its associated documents; they were also touched upon in the Wheatley Report. The Layfield Committee also examined in depth the field of local taxation, and its relationship to the complex of taxes available from time to time to central government. It can be assumed as a working hypothesis that local government will continue to be financed from a mix of local taxation and central financial aid, the proportions being dependent on the contemporary political muscle, the range of local functions, the movements in local and general public expenditure in Scotland, and the ability of the existing or any new local government areas to operate other local taxes which may — should the powers be conferred — become available. For example, it is normally accepted that a local income tax would be administratively and technically practicable only if applied over large local government areas. The total funds to be allocated and distributed to Scottish local government by the Assembly will be a matter for the Assembly itself, due regard being paid — one assumes — to the local government element included in the Block Grant awarded by Westminster to the Assembly to cover its overall financial needs. The ultimate outcome of the effect of these complex factors is uncertain, but a new equilibrium will not be reached without a wrangle.

Leaving aside the global financial and local taxation aspects, demands for changes in local government would apply to the remaining elements in local government — areas, status and functions. The analysis of potential areas undertaken by the Wheatley Commission detected five levels, of which two (region and district) were selected for the now standard mainland structure of local government. The major results of this basically two-tier system were firstly, the hope (if no more) of economies of scale in the operation of the services placed with the upper regional tier, and secondly, the inevitable new remoteness far greater than anything experienced in the former structure. Before reorganisation, Scottish local government included a very large proportion of very small local authorities (if size is measured by population served) many of which had a long and proud history. The new structure with only sixty-two mainland authorities has meant that, in comparison with their predecessors, all the authorities are large whatever test be applied. The Wheatley Commission foresaw this feature, but their proposed remedy of the community council has not silenced the critics of 'remote' local government. The inflation in Britain which gathered momentum at the time of the reform of local government produced sharply rising levels of expenditure which, at a minimum, cast further doubts on the economies which the new local government units were expected to demonstrate. The end products of many of the local services are intangible and cannot respond readily (as yet) to a quantative analysis designed to test the efficiency and effectiveness of their provision. Thus the operational advantages of the new authorities are neither blindingly obvious nor readily investigated, whereas the defects caused by the new territorial and population sizes of the authorities are widely felt.

The creation of the new larger authorities automatically widened the area of charge over which the regional, and often the district, rate is levied. Individual ratepayers sometimes found themselves meeting a higher rate bill in real terms without any concurrent improvement in the standard of local services or the facilities supplied. The most obvious example occurred in rural areas where the levy of the regional rate helps to finance services which may either be absent in the particular locality or appear to have but little relevance to local needs.

The effects of inflation on local government costs, and the doubts about the technical efficiencies of the new authorities, underpin the concern about the effect on individuals of the increases in rates caused by the distribution of expenditures over the new wider areas, and each factor adds its quota of pressure to the wish for a return to the generally smaller, more local, local government of the past. The main targets for attack are the larger regions, and notably the Strathclyde region which illustrates the features described above more than most, though the protagonists for the disbandment of the regional tier do not limit their campaign to any one region.

The investigation of areas made by the Wheatley Commission had a depth which their investigation of functions lacked. The problem is, admittedly, much more speculative in nature. While there is a general agreement that some local services require large areas, or large populations, or both, for their effective and efficient provision, there is no agreement about the meaning of 'large' nor is there any sign that agreement is possible or imminent. Recourse is then had to judgment, experience and other subjective tests rather than an objective and quantified analysis. A good deal of informed evidence to the Wheatley Commission commented adversely on the inappropriateness of the then existing small areas of service provision, and this was reflected in the recommended division of functions as between region and district, and in the desire for larger authorities. It is probable, though incapable of demonstration, that there is little real disagreement about the general pattern of distribution of functions and services — the education, police and fire services, for example, are hardly operationally suitable to a small district council while the placing of the environmental health function at regional level has not been seriously canvassed.

There are, however, specific problems connected with the present arrangements and these cannot be swept under the carpet. The rejection of the Wheatley recommendation that housing should be a regional service — however well-intended that rejection may have been — has led to policy and operational problems as between region and districts. The concurrent and shared planning powers and duties, and the concurrent powers in regard to leisure and recreation with the regional supervisory role which accompanies them, add force to the stresses and strain produced by jurisdictional boundaries and functional overlap. Although the problems can be minimised by devices such as liaison committees to promote policy integration and operational coherence, the statutory division of functions tends to institutionalise the fragmentation and highlight the differences between the two tiers of authorities. The main area of difficulty must lie in the policy-making levels of local government.

The division of function also leads to confusion in the mind of the public. No doubt as knowledge and understanding of the new system and arrangements grow, the confusion will diminish but it is unlikely to vanish. The demise of the former most-purpose authorities — the counties of cities of Aberdeen, Dundee, Edinburgh and Glasgow — and the creation of new most-purpose authorities in the shape of the islands authorities of Orkney, Shetland and the Western Isles at the other end of the population range, demonstrate that the principle of the single-tier authority has not been abandoned but stood on its head. Again, it is in the former counties of cities where the difficulties of disentangling the new division of functions was felt most. The 'one-door' principle, which envisages a single local channel through which all public involvement with the whole complex of local government services (and possibly other services such as local health) would operate, is still an ideal and not a practicality.

The arguments about the placing of the large-scale and small-scale services are mainly at the level of the operating efficiencies, but there is also the overriding policy-making dimension to be taken into account. The criticism about the remoteness of the councillor in large local government is paralleled by a criticism of remote policy-making, operational co-ordination and general decision-making. It appears to be often assumed that the only way in which a local function, especially those involving a high degree of personal service to the public, such as social work, can be related closely to the needs of a number of local communities is by way of small authority responsibility. The trend in recent decades towards operational decentralisation coupled with regional guidelines on policy is either ignored or denied, the solution sought being the abolition of the regions and the upgrading of the districts, irrespective of other important factors to be taken into account such as costs, staffing, and the impact of the interrelated functions. The arguments tend to be emotional, not rational, and often ignore the very serious defects of reliance upon joint committees and boards.

Hence the 'reformers', commonly wearing the guise of the abolishers of the regions, draw upon several arguments: general remoteness; an unwarranted shift of financial burden through the regional rate; doubts about the operational efficiency and effectiveness; and an imperative to couple narrowly-viewed local needs with locally determined policies and locally controlled operations.

Further claims for another reorganisation can be lodged by the districts. The fifty-three district councils have a slender range of functions, reduced still more for those in the remoter regions, and local government cannot thrive without worthwhile tasks for councillors and appropriate opportunities and careers for the staffs. The glory of the counties of cities has vanished, and shifts of power and responsibilities of that kind cannot occur without some dismay and bitterness, and an understandable urge to return to the past.

Allowing for recognition of the high (if unknown) cost of another reorganisation, for the inevitable adverse reaction by all the staffs involved, and for the overbrief time which has elapsed for any proper appraisal of the Wheatley system in actual operation, too much has already been linked with the creation of the Assembly to assume that the articulated dislike of the present system will fade away. The possibilities of change must be assessed.

Government is about power, and a revised local government system working with the Assembly will reflect the new structuring of devolved power. The crucial factors are the attitude to be adopted by the Assembly in viewing its own activities, and — in consequence, — what is to be passed to, left with, or transferred from, local government. The role of the Assembly cannot be dissociated from that of local government for each must cover a good deal of ground which is of interest to the other. Although from most viewpoints what is given to local government can be seen as a residual, i.e., what is left when the functions of the higher level bodies have been decided upon, the process of determining this is one of interaction not of edict.

Definitions of local government avoid offering any precise meaning of the term 'local', and the first question to decide is whether the taking on by the Assembly itself of any existing local government function would continue to endow that function with 'local' significance, and what effect this shift would have. The allocation of the services and functions placed with local government from time to time does not respond to objective analysis; the pattern is the result of a variety of expediencies adopted by Parliament from time, and modified in the light of various pressures. There is no inherent rationality in the location of the services and functions which have been placed with the public sector as a whole, but a good deal of emotion. Arguments can easily be marshalled to advocate with great persuasiveness the transfer of a number of services to, or from, local government.

The Wheatley Commission rejected evidence exploring an 'all-Scotland' solution to the allocation of certain major functions.

Evidence from a number of professional bodies and other persons advocated the removal of those services and functions which were their peculiar concern from the local authorities to the central machinery, but their arguments did not sway the Commission. The transfer of local functions to the Assembly would certainly not strengthen local government in its historical context, and the defects currently identified with local government would be enlarged and encouraged if all policy and operational duties were shifted to the Assembly. Remote local government would become even remoter Assembly government on matters with a substantial local content.

Yet if the regions were to be disbanded, and the regional functions reallocated within the remaining local authorities, it is straining the intelligence to visualise currently accepted large-scale services such as the police and fire services being fragmented over fifty-three districts. If such a move were contemplated, recourse would be had to the discarded and much discredited system of joint committees and joint boards, with its inherent lack of public accountability for policies, operations and finance. It is equally difficult to see the local government educational responsibilities diffused over the whole range of district councils, or that those councils would want to take them on. The various aspects of the water supply system are manifestly unsuitable for small area provision, the arguments being if anything in the opposite direction on technical grounds. Of course, it is not necessary to have a uniform standardised local government system throughout Scotland, but a variegated pattern would not aid public comprehension, nor make the task of the Assembly any easier. Also, the financial consequences of this approach would need close prior investigation. If the regions were to be disbanded, some of the major functions would have to be transferred to the Assembly or other arrangements made for *ad hoc* agencies to be created. In either case, suitable machinery for administering the services would be required, and this would have to be staffed, and monitored by the Assembly. The Assembly's role would become substantially executive and operational, not deliberative and legislating.

The ability of the Scottish Secretary to enter into agreements with other public bodies, allowing the latter to act as agencies, appears to permit certain central Assembly functions to be devolved operationally to the local authorities. In this event, it would be possible to increase the range of local authority executive responsibilities on a reimbursable basis, and enlist another argument in favour of maintaining local government, especially the major authorities. This line of thought cannot be pursued until the tasks to be adopted by the Assembly have become clarified and the future of the *ad hoc* agencies and the NHS has been determined.

For many years local authorities have acted collectively through the medium of associations of local authorities, formerly set up for each type of authority. With reorganisation, a review of the arrangements was necessary and finally one single powerful local authority association emerged — COSLA, the Convention of Scottish Local Authorities. The two-tier system of local government, the impact of the massive Strathclyde Region, and the special features of the Islands areas, provide opportunities for conflict and dissent which may now have to be resolved within COSLA rather than by the Scottish Office. Thus, COSLA is now the formal spokesman for Scottish local government.

COSLA is not only the obvious channel of communication between the Assembly and the Scottish Office, but it has a statutory role to perform as a body to be consulted by the Secretary of State, and his successors in the Assembly, on a variety of matters including the annual round of talks on grants to local government. The process of consultation is a real one, and continuous. COSLA is not a directly elected body. It is not answerable to the public for what is said in its name, nor are its proceedings and deliberations under the same scrutiny as applies to the local authorities whom it represents. Nonetheless, it can lay claim to a vast mass of expertise and knowledge, and has an obvious right to offer views on local government matters which are valid as — and possible more informed than — those of the Assembly.

Irrespective of any kind of fundamental changes in the structure, functions and areas of local government, the internal organisation and management processes of the Assembly must have an interface, and interact, with the local authorities with whom the Assembly works. Channels of communication between the Assembly, and the local authorities and COSLA, must be forged and kept in working order. These requirements bring into focus the possibility of a shift of role on the part of the pressure groups and political parties who operate in and through local government. The pre-Assembly arrangements in the central machinery, involving the Commons, the Scottish Grand Committee, the Scottish Standing Committees, the Scottish Office, and the five Scottish Departments, all tended to concentrate the main Parliamentary activity on debates on principles and questions about details — with occasional debates about details.

An important element in the demand for the Assembly lies in a

progressive extension of the opportunities to debate all aspects of
Scottish affairs in a localised forum. The organisation adopted by the
Assembly to enable debates of the required quality and depth to take
place is likely also to open up for discussion in the Assembly many
matters which are currently examined either less searchingly in Parliament at Westminster or in minute detail in primarily local terms in the
council chambers and committee rooms of local authorities. The
committee system adopted by the Assembly, with the functional
boundaries of the committees which are unlikely to reflect (except
fortuitously) the committee remits inside local authorities, will
determine the kind of dialogue which will emerge between the local
authorities and COSLA on the one hand, and the 'Minister', the
'Department' and the Assembly committee chairman on the other.

The coexistence of the Assembly and the present form of local
government is certain to be criticised on the grounds of 'over-govern-
ment'. The same argument can be applied to the committees of the
Assembly if they become immersed in the kind of detail thought more
appropriate (or more traditional) to local authorities. The price to be
paid for more public participation through the Assembly could be
confusion about responsibility, delay in decisions, and tedious repetition
in debates. The weight of local government duties has increased
embarrassingly since 1945 — a process often fostered by Parliament
without any real thought of the total consequences — and the activities
of local authorities are socially interventionist and widespread.
Although local policy-making takes place within the limits conferred
by legislation, the policies and operations of local authorities are as
much a matter of differences of opinion as are those of central
government, and often of greater immediate significance for individuals.
If the postbag of the members of the Assembly should resemble that of
the Westminster Members of Parliament for Scottish constituencies,
with its mass of correspondence on contentious local issues, there will
be a great temptation to seek yet another rehearsal of the policies and
practices of local authorities and a fresh chance for those who disagree
with a local decision to get it changed or overturned. In short, the
Assembly could easily misdirect itself about its role in local government affairs, by becoming another local authority with national
dimensions, unless steps are taken to prevent this by clear remits to
the Assembly committees and a strict interpretation of the rules of
debate.

It is frequently asserted that local authorities are already under the
firm and detailed control of central government and have little room

for manoeuvre in relation to policy or day to day activities. This view is too extreme to be valid, but areas of central control and guidance can, and must, exist. It would be tempting for the Assembly to continue this situation, and to criticise and seek to influence local authority decisions, whether or not specific statutory powers allowed them to do so. It is scarcely possible to visualise an effective and energetic Assembly which would be content to debate issues fundamental to the social and economic welfare of Scotland without calling into question the detailed policies of local authorities. Local authorities are the state agencies most widely used by Parliament and central government for implementing national policies. Bearing this in mind, and recalling the large share of the Block Grant which will be given to the Assembly and passed on to local authorities for spending decisions, there can be no doubt that local government matters will be under sustained scrutiny by the Assembly as a matter of course.

The emergence of the Assembly must thus call into question the ability of an active local government, and a central policy-making and investigatory body, to co-exist unless there is a very precise delineation of the respective powers and duties, and strong self-discipline on the part of the Assembly. The creation of a new and higher level participatory forum for pressure groups and political parties to criticise local authorities, or give more muscle to efforts to persuade them to change their decisions, will not bring fresh life into local government but emasculate it. The search for competent members of the Assembly may thin the ranks of those who serve local government at the present time, and people of the necessary capacity will not be attracted to serve as councillors in any kind of local authority if the issues are really debated, determined and monitored at Assembly level.

This line of argument may be thought to add weight to those who seek to abolish the regions, since the move of regional functions to the Assembly would get rid of the conflict between region and district, but the factors apply equally to district councils, particularly if their range of functions were widened. The number of local authorities is no longer a material factor since no predictable amendment to the number of local authorities would restore the pre-1975 scene of over four hundred local authorities with varying powers, and the possibility of divide and rule. The dangers for the future of local government where a new central machine is set up with potential administrative and operational powers as well as major policy-making duties can be seen in the disappearance of the traditional form of local government in Northern Ireland.

New institutional relationships must occur. The Assembly with its internal structures of committees and so on — probably complex in practice though simple to describe — plus the continuing role of the Scottish Office, the UK interest in financial and other issues which have a profound significance for local government, has to be reconciled with a local government system still coming to grips with the effects of reorganisation in a hostile climate.

No doubt an early task for the Assembly will be to make a decision whether to review Scottish local government as an immediate or a long-term objective. To select the former would be disastrous; the latter could be embarked upon after the Assembly has put its own house in order. Continued vigilance on the part of all with the interests of local government at heart will be needed if it is not to be made unworkable as an unfortunate by-product of an Assembly whose *raison d'etre* is an improvement in the democratic processes in Scotland. The Assembly must not be made up of second-class MPs, nor local authorities with failed candidates for the Assembly. The initial task is to clarify the functions of each part of the government of Scotland, and this will take time, patience, and a commitment to preserve the identity and importance of local government.

Chapter 12

Intermediate Government

DESMOND MISSELBROOK

THIS essay considers certain matters which may affect, for better
or worse, existing practical activities of importance to the progress
and well-being of the community. Constitutional change can generate
elation, even euphoria; it can liberate enthusiasm, questioning and
inventiveness. It can promote novelty and activity, but it can also
evoke anxiety and uncertainty. As it takes place the world will not
stand still. It does not help to indicate a route by suggesting that the
traveller has started from the wrong place. Existing plans and commitments must inevitably go on and uncertainty at a time of social and
economical difficulty can be damaging. There is an inherent conflict. A
creative solution is the art of the able administrator and statesman. The
realisation of this art is part of the challenge.

The expectations of the electorate may be high, even extravagant.
Expectations beyond the potentiality for fulfilment lead to disillusion-
ment, which is a stultifying condition. To enthuse but not over excite
will be a test of this leadership, but change for the sake of change seems
to be a common disorder of governments.

The earlier essays have been concerned with the constitutional,
administrative, and political activities of governing and have been
based on a depth of experience in these activities or the study of them.
This chapter deals with a rather different group of people and activities.
The people in the main have never sought political election, nationally
or locally, or if they have, they are not in this connection acting
politically. The great majority would also not have been engaged in the
provision of skilled administrative services for national or local governments. Most would not have pursued in depth formal studies in
constitutional and political matters. They would have earned their
living in commerce, industry or a profession and would additionally
have accepted appointments to specialised Advisory Committees or

Boards of various kinds such as for Health, Training, New Towns, Neddies and so on. These Committees or Boards are part of organisations set up to achieve certain broad purposes and the task for the members is a-politically and uncontroversially, but without sterility, to assist the effective achievement of these purposes. The posts are by appointment. The deliberations are private and the minutes are confidential. But the results of these deliberations are explicitly public and subject to comment and assault from all points of the community compass. The holders of these appointments, some of which are held in an honorary capacity, are predisposed to consider the organisations both socially constructive and democratic in character. Yet there is widespread concern about political patronage, about the scrutiny of appointments and about accountability. There are calls for new kinds of elections, for all meetings to be public and for all minutes to be published. There is also some sense of oppression from the apparently ever-increasing multiplicity of bodies whose purposes are but little understood. At the same time, there is also a growing public cynicism about elected representatives and frequent questioning of their motives and honesty of purpose. Such contradictions are perhaps symptoms of a nation which is anxious and confused about where it is going and uncertain about its values. Constitutional change can either give new positive purposefulness or exacerbate anxiety. The change itself does not produce new purposefulness; this has to be worked for.

Against this background what does the given title of this paper mean? Does it mean anything at all? The logical answer must be that it does not mean very much yet it obviously does not 'feel' absurd. Intermediate is 'in-between'; but in-between what and what? Governments are elected or imposed according to constitutional, statutory or arbitrary arrangements. For us in a democracy, government is by election. The title cannot have meaning as 'elected in-between'; does it mean 'imposed in-between'? If so, there are a great number of such impositions.

This is the realm of 'Quangos' — quasi-autonomous non-government organsations. 'Quango', with its zoological connotation of an ill-formed and ridiculous beast has become a symbol of mistrust. But 'quasi' is 'as if' and very many of these bodies to which the term 'Quango' is applied are in no way 'as if'. They are statutory bodies responsible themselves in a variety of public ways for their own actions. If the emphasis is to be upon 'as if autonomous' this cannot refer to an absence of accountability because in most cases this is clearly defined. It perhaps refers to a feeling among Members of

Parliament and members of the public that information is not so conveniently obtained as by a question to a Minister or other elected representatives. These organisations are however usually only too glad to answer queries because of the interest exhibited. The uneasiness might refer to the fact that meetings are, for good reason, held in private although the results are public.

The title is used to cover that great multiplicity of bodies and agencies which, with his customary lucidity and succinctness, was recently surveyed by Sir Douglas Haddow. He teased out the main components and therefore perhaps will not be too offended if they are further summarised into five groups:

1. Expert advisory committees and councils to which are invited a wider range of experts than a Government Department could reasonably have available and which give opportunities for wide consultation.

2. Agencies with executive powers to run on behalf of the Secretary of State for Scotland to whom they are answerable, such organisations as the fifteen Health Boards in Scotland or, as another example, specialist educational institutions.

3. Regulatory and sometimes marketing bodies such as, for example, the Milk Marketing Board or the White Fish Authority.

4. Economic development agencies such as the Scottish Development Agency, the Highlands and Islands Development Board, the Tourist Board and the five Development Corporations for the Scottish New Towns.

5. Scottish Boards which are essentially area Boards of United Kingdom nationalised industries such as the Scottish Tele-communications Board, the Postal Board, the Hydro Electric Board and others.

These bodies taken together cover wide aspects of life in Scotland, they attract much expertise and experience, invite wide participation on an appointed or nominated basis and they may administer significant amounts of public money. They may also have an influence on broad aspects of policy. Some may have been set up primarily to parallel a similar body established south of the border. They must inevitably vary in cost and/or administrative effectiveness.

The Advisory bodies in their simplest form provide expert opinion and are modes of consultation. They can develop into pressure groups or, in their grandest form, namely as a Commission, become instruments of procrastination. Generally they seem to have been regarded as valuable and have not been the object of public concern. A newly elected Assembly with much to sort out might therefore not be expected to give early attention to these bodies except in one eventuality. If the working arrangements of the Assembly follow the pattern suggested by John Mackintosh, the committees could initially question whether they could not themselves provide the advisory functions and thus make the existence of such bodies redundant. Each case would have to be considered on its merits in terms of the specialist knowledge required because, basically, success in being elected does not illustrate any other skill than that of becoming elected. The most difficult cases would be those in which an advisory body was becoming a pressure group. It would then be seen to trespass into the province of the elected representatives which is to promote policy.

The Scottish Boards of nationalised industries are really area Boards of a United Kingdom Authority and as such can be set aside. This does not ignore their proven value. There is ample evidence to show that in the sensing of local need, in increased effectiveness and job satisfaction as a result of decentralisation, through the examination of existing practices, often with help of non-executive members, they have not only improved the local performance but also made significant contributions to the thinking of their parent bodies.

The Regulatory Bodies for professional matters and professional conduct are primarily areas for the expert although they can periodically arouse wide public interest if their deliberations have an impact on deeply held beliefs or values or if, as with accounting for inflation, the debate has seemed to throw the accounting profession into disarray.

The other regulatory and marketing organisations have in part to be considered in relation to the United Kingdom as a whole. But, in so far as they propose policies or courses of action which affect Scottish interests, an Assembly would clearly have a lot to say, and there is bound to be a strong lobby. When the Assembly is elected there would have to be a period of adjustment and working out of relationships with these bodies.

We are left now with the Health Boards and the various bodies associated with them and lastly with the group which has been called development agencies.

The provision of health services is a very sensitive, complex and costly activity. It is first of all sensitive because it can affect each one of us so intimately and secondly because of the professional sensitivities of those who care for us. To what extent will these areas of sensitivity be affected by the existence of an Assembly?

The Assembly will not have control over the pay or structure of the medical profession but it will have control over the structure and operation of the Health Service. It will have control of policy on private practice, contraception, transplant surgery and the use of dead bodies. Occupational health and the control of drugs will be outside its control. It will, however, determine how much money is to be spent on health care and it will select the priorities for such spending.

The professional status and emoluments of the medical profession will be decided elsewhere but patient and doctor alike will have an interest in the amount of money to be allocated to health services and the priorities which are determined; and both of these are within the powers of the Assembly.

The Health Service is complex partly by its very nature and partly as a result of the structure which has been evolved. The Assembly will have complete control of the structure and can, therefore, examine the effectiveness of the existing arrangements. One must suppose, and this is said with great respect to the splendid work which has been done by the Health Service, it would be the duty of the Assembly to satisfy itself whether or not it was happy with the way things are now done and to consider what changes, if any, it would wish to make. To take an extreme example, it might decide that because of the size of the Scottish population, the fact that hospital provision has always been dealt with by the Department of Health and because of the existing responsibility of government officers to answer questions on expenditure, the service could be better run by a government department and that much of the existing structure could be dispensed with. The argument would be that existing arrangements may have been appropriate south of the border or for the UK as a whole but not for Scotland with a devolved Assembly.

The same kind of questioning can be expected in respect of New Town Development Corporations. Should the individual Boards be abolished and all the towns be run by the officials whose activities would be co-ordinated by the SDA or by a government department? It will be argued later that this might not be a very good idea but the inevitability of this kind of questioning must be faced. Organisations were created for the UK as a whole and with the bulk of the population south of the border. Do the arrangements for fifty million people suit five million people? For these bodies to be paranoid about questioning would be as useless as for committees of the Assembly to be arrogant inquisitors.

There is, however, one general question which can now be raised. Devolution is intended to give greater local control, to increase participation and enhance confidence. Is it possible that decentralisation to Scotland could lead to a greater centralisation within Scotland and this in the names of efficiency and cost effectiveness?

We turn now to economic Development Agencies namely, the SDA, the HIDB, the five New Town Development Corporations and the Scottish Tourist Board.

It is important to stress again that these are agencies of Government and they are not part of Government in the political and elected sense. They are not politically partisan. Apart from the SDA which is very new, they have continued under successive administrations of different political character and their appointed members have been re-appointed by politically different administrations. They are executive bodies with moderately clear terms of reference which can be interpreted with a modest degree of flexibility but in close liaison with officials of the Scottish Office who are always readily available and quick and constructive in response. They have quite large executive staffs some of whom are, in specific cases, members of the Board of the agency. In other instances the Board is composed of appointed non-executive members only. All of these persons are at present ultimately responsible to the Secretary of State for Scotland. The responsibility for these agencies will be devolved to the Assembly but economic and industrial guidelines will continue to be set by the Secretary of State.

All these agencies are concerned with economic development and employment and in differing but significant ways with the quality of life in Scotland. In this connection it is, perhaps, useful to recall that when the debate started south of the border, about the respective importance of urban regeneration and new town development, the Secretary of State for Scotland underlined as the primary purpose of Scottish New Towns their role as focal points of economic growth both regionally and for Scotland as a whole. Urban regeneration received too little attention in the past but the change of heart comes at a time of severe economic recession when nothing should be done which could interfere with organisations which have had any success in the attraction and creation of jobs.

Economic matters are of such pressing urgency that more must be said on this aspect of existing agencies and the Assembly. However, we should first consider the ground rules for agencies and advisory bodies if they are to perform effectively and command broad public confidence as creative institutions of an informed democracy.

(1) Organisations should periodically be reviewed to ensure that they are not self perpetuating when their usefulness has ceased.

(2) As a result of the dates and circumstances when different bodies were created it is necessary to watch for wasteful overlapping and incoherence.

(3) Appointments to these bodies should be, and be seen to be, relevant and preferably apt. Any suspicion that appointments were primarily a reward for past political or other services, a compensation for loss of an office or a hidden subsidy, destroys confidence in the organisations to which the appointments are made. At the same time, the methods of consultation and scrutiny which are used should be such as not to limit the field of choice. Those who have sufficient sense of public duty to undertake public appointments inevitably expose themselves to public comment. If the method of scrutiny of appointment is such as to be embarrassing to other organisations to which such individuals belong it could prohibit the availability of many able people.

(4) The social purposes of agencies and other bodies is determined by an elected body. These agencies have much to contribute to the development of thought about these purposes and to the methods of realising them but they do not set these goals for themselves.

A reference was made earlier to a new emphasis placed by the Secretary of State for Scotland on the role of New Town Development Corporations as focal points of economic growth. Associated with this economic target was a subsequent change of role by which the population overspill responsibilities of these Corporations was removed. This latter change was broad social policy whereas the former was an economic guideline. Such a combination of objectives may in future require careful consideration in respect of devolved and non-devolved powers.

Another example could be taken from the broad range of purposes of the SDA. It is required to improve working and living environments, protect employment in industries which are viable but under pressure, support innovation with exciting prospects but immediate risks, undertake risks which other financial institutions would not accept and achieve certain standards of return on investment. Such important activities range widely over devolved and non-devolved matters and present significant choices in priorities for the use of funds and the return on investments. Such choices must inevitably be the concern of an elected Assembly but at the same time the agency must be able effectively to carry out its tasks. This leads to the last of these ground rules.

(5) It is essential that many of the organisations we are considering

should be able to preserve confidentiality, to act with speed and enter into binding commitments as is required. This is particularly important for those engaged in attracting industry and jobs. These agencies are the executive organs of democracy. The democratic process itself will be more open and protracted and that is why it sets up these bodies, although it controls their social purposes and calls them to account.

Within guidelines and financial control the Assembly will have a say in economic development through HIDB, New Towns, Tourism and SDA. Social welfare, housing, education minus the universities, are also devolved. Employment is not devolved. This may be understandable as unemployment is a UK problem but it is a particularly serious one in Scotland and must therefore be a subject for deep concern within an Assembly.

Hobby horses are allowed to be ridden peaceably on the high road. It is therefore permissible to express the view that no political party, no organisation of employers or trades unionists, no professional body (e.g. BIM) has as yet been prepared to face up to the national crisis of present and potential levels of unemployment. It seems — and it would be agreeable to be wrong — that a very high level of unemployment will be with us for a very considerable time unless new ways of thinking and acting about the creation of employment are developed.

'Stop-go' was with us for so long that it has become, apparently, impossible for many to face the fundamental change which has taken place in our industrial situation and therefore to display the humility which admits that we really do not know how to solve a situation which, because it is wasteful and a social sickness, should be a concern for all citizens whatever their roles. Furthermore, this situation is also capable of obstructing many steps which will be necessary to revive the economy in the longer term. It could undermine competitiveness and modernisation. We cannot any longer export inflation and many of the steps which will have to be taken are likely to lead to further redundancy. There is, therefore, an urgent need for a co-operative national effort to adopt new attitudes and define new ways of creating socially useful employment. Industrial investment in existing and new industry is vital but this would take far too long to create sufficient new job opportunities. New attitudes are essential if anything is to be done. It is now more generally accepted that the creation of wealth by industry and commerce is not only essential but a socially responsible activity. If this is so then the creation of other socially useful occupations perhaps less directly concerned with the immediate creation of wealth may come to be regarded not just as a substitute for a real job but as a creative solution to our present difficulties.

Perhaps an Assembly, as a new body, might stimulate both a new awareness as well as action, but it means that there will be a need for a speedy appraisal of the relationship between economic development and employment and this will produce the odd paradox of giving primary attention to a matter which is not devolved.

There is also a negative side to this need for action. An Assembly should be careful to do nothing that might inhibit existing activities which are creating jobs. There are two besetting sins which a new organisation will need to resist. These are the desire to make change for the sake of change and secondly to spend so much time examining the sitting in judgment of what now exists that those who should be getting on with the job are instead spending all their time preparing for real or imagined inquests.

A Roman general of the first century wrote: 'We trained hard — but it seemed that every time we were beginning to form up into teams we would be re-organised. I was to learn later in life that we tend to meet any new situation by re-organising and a wonderful method it can be for creating the illusion of progress while producing confusion, inefficiency and demoralisation'.

It is a common disorder of Governments and some commercial organisations to become obsessed with organisational change as a substitute for the solving of problems. Successive Governments seem to feel a need to make new organisational arrangements in order to give an appearance of difference and to show that something is happening. The hope is somehow nourished that in the process the problem will be solved or disappear. Administrative change to give effect to an already determined solution to a problem is one thing. Change for the sake of change, however fervent the hope, is nothing.

Possibly an Assembly might achieve, in the economic field, what has happened in the field of foreign policy. This is the creation of sufficient common ground between the parties so that practical agencies may be able consistently to get on with a job for a period of years. This would be a most significant step forward. Wars have forced this kind of co-operation between political parties; foreign policy has frequently invited such co-operation; economic development cries out for it.

The second sin is an obsession with examination, enquiry and appraisal. The role of watchdog in respect of social goals and accountability is vital in a democracy. However, responsibility in the scrutineers is also vital to an effective democracy. One hundred and fifty members of a new Assembly would be less than human if they were not anxious to make their mark. Not to damage what is working will call for much courage and self-control.

Any new body is likely to be somewhat self-conscious about its administrative arrangements and it can pursue a theoretically desirable search for tidiness. Tidiness and effectiveness however, do not necessarily march hand in hand. It would be perfectly possible, for example, to devise on paper arrangements for the other development agencies to be run by the Scottish Development Agency — indeed its name almost invites this — or for all the agencies to be run by a Government Department. This would look logical and could also get round the problems of elected representatives. The untidiness of experience suggests that this could be a retrograde step. Industry and commerce cannot be directed as to where they will go and there are many suitors, some with more attractive financial inducements.

The individuality of separate organisations gives the potential employer a choice. Quite small matters or the feel of relationships can determine a choice. That is why, for example, the Scottish New Towns share a London office to attract companies to Scotland, but when an enquiry comes along they each put their goods in their own shop windows and try to make a sale. They are constantly aware that the competition is not primarily among themselves or with the other areas in Scotland. The competition is with England, Ireland, Wales and the continent of Europe.

This individuality is the individuality of a town or community and its way of life. The quality of life as developed and projected by a Development Corporation can be quite as compelling for an employer as the design of a factory or the geographical location of a place.

The attraction of companies and thereby jobs is a sophisticated and subtle process which projects a compelling image, acts with the speed and decision frequently not possible for committees, can ensure confidentiality, and can parade when necessary a diversity of expertise from its officials and from its non-executive members.

Job creation and economic development have to march in step with housing, education and social welfare. To attract industry and commerce it is first necessary to be able to offer buildings or sites. Factories are no use without houses. Houses are built for people who need social facilities and education. This calls for co-ordination of effort and there is plenty of experience south of the border how this has been done. But the handling of these matters with the Scottish Office has been far simpler and quicker, it can be argued, than arrangements which existed in the south and it would be a great tragedy if the effectiveness of these existing arrangements were to be lost through the creation, which is inevitable, of a variety of Departments without also affecting the arrangements for the necessary co-ordination.

We have deeply serious economic problems and the solutions are not exclusively or indeed primarily economic ones. They are more concerned with attitudes, values and the spiritual quality of life and here there is plenty of scope for leadership.